Better Late Than Early

Better Late Than Early

A New Approach to Your Child's Education

Raymond S. Moore
&
Dorothy N. Moore

READER'S DIGEST PRESS

Distributed by Hewitt Research Foundation
Berrien Springs, MI 49103, 1982

Library of Congress Cataloging in Publication Data

Moore, Raymond S
Better late than early.

Bibliography: p.
1. Readiness for school. 2. School age (Entrance age)
I. Moore, Dorothy N., joint author.
II. Title.
LB1132.M66   372.1'2'17   74–22275

Distributed by Hewitt Research Foundation
Berrien Springs, MI 49103, 1982
ISBN: 0–88349–048–X
Designed by The Etheredges

To our parents and our children

A Note About Documentation

Source references in the body of the text appear as numbers within parentheses. These numbers are keyed to the Bibliography (page 218), which is a complete list, arranged alphabetically by author, of all works referred to by the authors. For example, the sentence beginning: "Seth Low and Pearl Spindler (91) reported . . ." refers the reader to the following entry in the Bibliography:

91. LOW, SETH, and PEARL SPINDLER. *Child Care Arrangements of Working Mothers in the United States*. Washington, D.C.: Children's Bureau Publication No. 46, 1968.

Contents

FOREWORD 1   xi

FOREWORD 2   xiii

PROLOGUE   xv

PART I

1. Behind the Early Childhood Scene   3
2. Making the Laws   10
3. Some Common Fears and Questions   20
4. When They Are Ready for School   32
5. Developing Attachments   36
6. Opportunity for Parents   52
7. Time and the Senses   63
8. Learning to Reason   77

9. Comparing Early and Late Starters   88

10. Comparing Home and School Costs   100

PART II

INTRODUCTION   109

11. Birth to 18 Months   112

12. 1 Year to Age 3   129

13. Age 2½ to Age 5   147

14. Age 4 to Age 7   171

15. Age 6 to Age 8 or 9   191

SUMMARY AND RECOMMENDATIONS   204

ACKNOWLEDGMENT   216

BIBLIOGRAPHY   218

INDEX   231

Foreword 1

Raymond Moore's adult life has spanned several careers as a professional in the field of education. He has been a classroom teacher and an administrator. He has worked in public schools and in universities, has been superintendent of a school system, and has held responsible positions at the Federal level in relation to policy-formation and implementation. These experiences led him, through the years, to become increasingly aware of existing and increasing problems associated with, and introduced by "early education."

He has pursued these questions indefatigably, broadly, and in a scholarly way. His awareness of, and struggles to demonstrate, the deficits and dangers inherent in premature introduction of children to schools and to "school-like" situations (as contrasted with home and "parenting") are in an honorable tradition which boasts such disparate pioneers as Dewey, Spitz, Paget and Holt. His commitment to parents and the home as our primary educational base is further exemplified by his own life and work-style that have made his wife and his son partners in his own professional work.

Moore brings a wealth of evidence from a wide variety of sources to indicate that early schooling, although promoting (perhaps) earlier cognitive organization, introduces a host of fateful "iatrogenic" disturbances. Our knowledge of maturation, development, developmental stages, and critical developmental periods from the human, all support Moore's basic thesis. Spitz, in his wisdom, differentiated between "learning" and what he called "fundamental education."* The latter is also what Moore focuses-upon. Of what value is the educational process, if the very process, when prematurely introduced

*Spitz, R.A. "Fundamental Education." In *Play and Development,* edited by M.W. Piers. New York: W.W. Norton and Co., 1972.

within the unfolding epigenetic field, distorts the developing psychic structure so as to interfere with future education, and learning to live and learning to love, let alone learning to learn.

Moore points out that there are sound psychoeducational principles that are violated by one-sided focusing on "too early," that evidences of success are mixed and not strong, and that evidences of failure abound. He also draws upon burgeoning evidence from the maturational side, indicating that human developmental neurophysiology also supports, more and more, the contention that the system is not ready at age 4 to 6 for "early schooling" as generally conceived; he furthermore draws upon the growing suggestion that "too early" may also interfere with necessary consolidation of processes at the neurophysiological level. We suspect that many children with so-colled "specific learning disability" or "minimal brain dysfunction," etc., suffer from developmental disturbances originating in an overdose of "the wrong thing at the wrong time". . . truly, better late than early.

This is an important book for parents and for professionals. It warns, it offers alternatives, and it never loses sight of its main focus—the health, happiness and "fundamental education" of our children.

David R. Metcalf, M.D.
Associate Professor of Psychiatry
University of Colorado Medical Center

Foreword 2

This book is a welcome contribution to the field of early childhood education and one that I feel was badly needed. To undertake such a task as the Moores have, and to bring it to completion, required an enormous amount of effort, work and, no less important, similar doses of courage, wisdom and objectivity.

As they say, the E.C.E. field is characterized by much confusion and verbal cannibalism. This is typical of areas such as this one, where the amount of research, though extensive in relative terms, is simultaneously scanty when compared with what needs to be learned and what questions need to be answered. One expects a certain amount of controversy and disagreement, at least while the initial mist that characterizes what is essentially unknown clears. Unfortunately, that natural mist tends to become a thick pea-soup fog when we add to it the vested interests of politicians, citizens, educators, professionals, and other pressure groups.

One of the laudable aims of the authors is to clarify the issues and to attempt to examine those facts as are available at this time to serve the best interest of the helpless and passive victim of the argument—that is, the young child.

Anywhere else an objective, scientific examination of the best information and research available will dictate the ultimate course of action in any given direction. Yet this is hardly ever the case in regard to children. Politicians and society generally behave as if they knew all there is to know about their nature, their needs, their development, their potential capabilities, etc., but is must be said, as the authors do, that this simply is not true. The potential disservice to the child because of the above attitude is indeed frightening to say the least.

To remedy the above the authors have made an extensive review of the literature available and have strongly come out

—on that basis as well as on the basis of their professional experience and research—on the side that "it is better late than early," in terms of education. This may seem to many as a radical departure from the thinking and tendencies of recent years. But at the very least, we should pause and reflect on the evidence presented.

The book's value is further enhanced by its very lucid exposition and by the fact that a multidisciplinary approach to the problem was taken, combining the knowledge and findings of the educator, the neurophysiologist, the developmental psychologist, the child psychiatrist, the sociologist, the parent, etc.

Personally, though I occasionally disagree with some of the views presented, I gladly acknowledge that I found myself, after reading it, enlightened and enriched in many ways. I suspect the same will be true for many of its readers. I suspect too that the authors will receive a whole range of responses from their intended audience. Praise will be mixed with legitimate disagreement and further, with sheer abuse, even personal threats, unbelievable as this may seem to some. They will be uttered by the few who do not wish light thrown into the area and can only react to objectivity, logic and reason by emanating heat. I know the authors are well aware of this from past experience, and I know too that they will persist in their task guided by the courage of their scientific convictions.

Humberto Nagera, M. D.
Director of the Child Psycho-analytic Study Program,
Children's Psychiatric Hospital
University of Michigan Medical School

Prologue

This book is a result of research on the young child's mental development originally undertaken by the Hewitt Research Foundation as a background for a pioneer study in early childhood development. A number of research studies by brain specialists and by psychologists had suggested that the normal child's brain is not ready for sustained learning programs—until he is 8 to 10 years of age. Some specialists doubted even then he should be forced into school. This was a surprising note, considering the nationwide trends toward early schooling.

For our own original research at the Hewitt Foundation where we functioned as a developmental psychologist and as a reading specialist, we decided to ask leading brain specialists and psychologists to study the same groups of children to see if their independent conclusions would be similar. These groups, basically lower and middle class in socioeconomic origin, included 15 to 30 children each, equally divided by sex with a range of 3 to 9 years. Specialists at the National Institute of Child Health and Human Development suggested that Dr. David Metcalf of the University of Colorado Medical School be appointed to lead such a study, and he accepted our invitation. Meanwhile, such an investigation required a prior screening of related research.

As we began systematically to review studies of the brain and perception, related research areas cried for attention, including some that had been largely ignored by educational planners. These gaps, we found, had led to serious misconceptions by many educators about such things as maternal attachment and deprivation, comparative school-entrance-age and parental attitudes. Moreover, we found that the existing research clearly supported the brain specialists and the psychologists in their contention that children are not ready for sustained learning programs until ages 8 to 10.

This does not mean that all authorities agree on all details. There are many variables not yet identified in early childhood research, and much work remains to be done. Nevertheless, we noted remarkable coincidences strongly suggesting that readiness for school seldom, if ever, comes before the ages of 8 to 10. This stirred us on to an even broader and deeper research review—and a harder look at the basic principles of childhood development.

The result is this book. While it is not the first work to suggest specific ages for the growing child's readiness for school, we disclose here a new and, we believe, practical version of a truth that has been intuitive to many parents and teachers. We call it the *integrated maturity level* (IML), because it concerns the child's maturation in

developmental areas such as vision, hearing, social-emo-
tional progress and the activities of the central nervous
system. When the normal child has become reasonably
mature enough in each and all areas so he can learn well
without serious mental or physical strain—usually not
before age eight—he has reached his IML and is ready for
school. The abnormal or handicapped child will, of
course, require special clinical help, and the deprived
child may often need special care outside the home
before he is eight.

We have published some of our findings previously in
articles and reports that appeared in both the popular and
professional press. In response, we received several thousand letters, most of which fell into three categories.
Many correspondents simply asked for more information;
some scholars, planners and parents voiced deep hurt or
concern at our position, but for every correspondent who
disagreed with us, more than five expressed concurrence
with our findings. Among these were leading early childhood education (ECE) specialists. Moreover, many parents and people involved in preschool work wrote that
they were grateful to find scientific support for ideas they
had long held, but which had been shaken by popular
pressures.

Nevertheless, if some educators and bureaucrats
have their way, most of our boys and girls will be taken
from us at age three or earlier and placed in tax-supported
preschools. Proponents of such programs promise that the
children will be better citizens. These men and women
appear to be sincere, but research indicates that they are
sincerely wrong. Unfortunately, they have made little use
of sound research, clearly indicating that such educational
planning would be at the children's expense and that the
tax bill for these programs would be enormous.

One question has been raised repeatedly in response

to our articles, "If it is not wise to send our children to school early, what suggestion do you have for giving children proper care in the home in order to insure their best development?" It is primarily to answer this question that this book was written.

Part I of this volume presents some of the background of the ECE dilemma, spells out key research facts, provides some idea of their interrelationships and offers suggestions based on the research data. (Many ECE specialists differentiate between preschool, day care and nursery school; however, we generally refer to them as out-of-home care.) Part II of the book, based on the detailed study and experience of many parents, describes what best can be done at home for the child during his first eight to ten years.

We are also asked frequently, "Why are you against preschool and day care?" Some people allege that we are against children, teachers and even schools. We feel like the mother who was accused of being unsympathetic with her toddlers when she kept them home from a party during a serious influenza epidemic.

It should be carefully noted in reading this volume that there is much need for day care. We do not dismiss day care or preschool out of hand. Special educators have worked with preschool and day-care planners to make excellent provision for deprived and handicapped youngsters, and we sanction early out-of-home education for these children whenever necessary.

We should also note two other assumptions that are commonly held, though both are also false: (1) that deprived or handicapped youngsters come only or mostly from ghetto homes, and (2) that poor families are not good families. It cannot be said with any certainty that more problems come from the poor than from the rich. It is the parent's quality of heart and his common sense that produces values in a child, not how much money the family has. Nevertheless, we feel there is no justification for ignoring poverty—it is one of society's first obligations to help the poor. But we do not assume that we must provide (or exclude) one type of institution—home or school—for one stratum of society. Thus we do ask some questions:

If one element of our society has a problem requiring a particular remedy, must we necessarily provide it for all?

Do we have the altruistic character to spend public money on those less fortunate without demanding the same services for ourselves?

Do we use the preschool primarily as a convenience for our own freedom, or do we view it as vital to our children?

Are we determined to solve the problems of our children on the basis of scientific evidence? Or do we prefer to operate by social pressure and shaky intuition?

In short, are we willing to reexamine our traditional ideas and to make difficult changes involving long-range sacrifices if they mean the eventual enrichment of the lives of our children and our society? On the basis of many studies of parent responses, we believe that most mothers and fathers will answer *Yes.*

For those who will, our findings will be of special interest. From our research and our studies, we have concluded that:

(1) The home is the primary institution for young children.

(2) We doubt the need for preschool for the larger segment of our population.

(3) We see the home as potentially more cost effective than the school for developing young children, and we find that projected governmental preschool programs may be so costly as to ruin the whole early childhood movement.

(4) We fear that planners may move too far too fast

without responsible reference to research.

(5) We acknowledge that the handicapped and seriously deprived may need special help out of home.

Subsequent to our first report, a number of diverse researchers, analysts, and commentators have published reviews largely consistent with our findings.

If you are sure that you know exactly what your child needs, or if you are more interested in your personal "freedoms" than you are in your children, this book may make you uncomfortable. On the other hand, if you are involved in the education of your children—and if you care about the quality of education in your community—this book should be helpful.

In either event, if, after such a reading, you find any research contrary to the evidence and conclusions reported here, we will be in your debt if you will send it to us.

R.S.M. and D.N.M.
Tudor Road at the Lake
Berrien Springs, Michigan 49103

Part I

1.

Behind the Early Childhood Scene

The family and the home are the foundation of our society. Whatever the shifting theories of child development, the importance of the family and the home has never been obliterated. What the child needs most to grow well is a warm one-to-one relationship with a parent (or parent figure) who is always there to comfort and guide him. During the first crucial eight years, home should be the child's only nest and parents the teachers for their children. These are the years when the child requires affection and emotional security more than learning skills, when he should be able to get ready for life unfettered by school rules.

There are exceptions to our home-care thesis, of course—glaring ones. And they include, perhaps, as many as 20 to 25% of our children. The *handicapped* child—

blind, crippled, spastic or deaf, who deserves the best clinical help we can find. The *disadvantaged* child, the prisoner of the ghetto or the mountain hollow, whose life must be enriched. The *deprived* child, whether he lives in a tenement or a mansion, whose parents are indifferent to, or overly indulgent, or ignorant of his needs. The *normal* child whose mother is forced by stark financial need to work for a living outside the home. Many, if not all, of these children should be given out-of-home care in environments that substitute for homes as closely as possible. We cannot overstress the importance of a home-like atmosphere, where adults respond warmly to children. In Switzerland, where children are normally thought to receive the best possible preschool care, Marie Meierhofer (98), director of a Zurich clinic, studied 500 babies in the city day nurseries. She found that ". . . many of the children were apathetic, had facial expressions of compressed lips and wrinkled foreheads, and cried and covered their eyes when approached." These signs of depression Dr. Meierhofer blamed almost entirely on isolation or lack of personal care. Thus, for the great majority of children, their own homes are still the best places for their early care.

Parents, by and large, are deeply concerned for the welfare of their children. Many of them will make sacrifices to insure their youngsters' good. But there are those who do not hide their urge to get "the kids" out from under their feet. They welcome any idea, neighborhood pressure or legislation that offers release and allows them to send their children to kindergarten or nursery school.

Yet it is more a denial of motherhood—and fatherhood—to unnecessarily send youngsters away from home before they are ready. Some parents say all they want is a little freedom or they simply have too much to do. So it is a question of parental values: Who and what comes first—parents' liberty or their children's welfare? True freedom implies responsibility to protect another person's liberties. If the young child develops best at home, then it is the greater loss for him, and ultimately for society, if he is sent elsewhere.

Many families, of course, reflect our technological and mobile society with its shifting environments and life styles. There is the current and widely circulated myth that the family is no longer a viable institution and should be shelved. Couple that myth with the sharply increased number of mothers working outside the home and it is no wonder that family life has become less and less secure. Unsettled parents with unsettled children reach out for some kind—any kind—of help or assurance. Families suffering from low self-esteem or lack of sound information are offered assistance by many kinds of business and professional people. Some of these sources do have wisdom and deep concern for children's developmental needs. But others are ready to take the parents' place for a few hours, or a day or a week simply for profit. Ultimately, all these factors display far less concern for children than for adults. Yet it is the little children who are far more vulnerable.

Another serious influence on the family has been those professionals who insist that to deny preschool experience to the normal child is educationally and psychologically unsound. But such people commonly make a basic assumption that is not true. They assume that the rapid development of a young child's intellect requires stimulation of a school-type program.

Such reasoning has resulted largely from Dr. Benjamin Bloom's famed conclusion that ". . . in terms of intelligence measured at age 17, from conception to age 4 the individual develops 50% of his mature intelligence" (14).

Learning psychologist Arthur Jensen (78), after carefully checking the Bloom report and applauding its more reliable aspects, specifically warns that finding half the statistical variance of adult intelligence by age 4 does not lead to the conclusion that people develop 50% of their mature intelligence by age 4. This is one of those instances in which statistical reasoning leads to an unwarranted conclusion.

Not only have Bloom's conclusions been misused, but they were not entirely sound in the first place. Nancy Bayley, University of California child psychologist from whose well-known studies Bloom obtained data and, in part, drew his conclusions, later noted (9) that Bloom's theory depends on an inadequate definition of intelligence as a unitary mental property. Actually, a child's "mature intelligence" at this period is not synonymous with understanding or ability to reason. It is, rather, a *potential ability* to reason or to understand. Yet Bloom's misleading conclusion constitutes one of the most frequent bases of recent preschool planning.

Many special interests are involved in the dispute over early childhood education; these interests range from substantial governmental investments to simple parental freedoms. There are commercial ventures in educational institutions, equipment, supplies and personnel; professional associations, political action groups, minority groups and labor unions; and a variety of other persons and groups caught up in the day-care and preschool movement. These vested interests have accomplished much good, but they should be placed in clear and firm perspective against two paramount goals: to insure the welfare of the child, including his optimum development; and to restore the unity and integrity of the family, providing parents with information on how to meet the developmental needs of their children. It is vital to implement these goals through programs that can be administered simply, with budgets that can be financed reasonably. If we place vested interests ahead of these interrelated goals, we risk the welfare and liberties of our children—a deprivation of the worst order.

In order to avoid such deprivation, parents must clearly understand the child's needs and how to relate to them. One of the principal skills of a successful teacher is understanding each child's state of readiness for a particular lesson or skill. Likewise, a good parent must have a knowledge of the child's maturing processes. Discussion of the child's maturity levels and when he is ready for school begins in Chapter 4. We call the coming together of his various maturities the IML, for integrated maturity level.

It is time to look at the facts instead of at the neighbors. Just because "everyone is doing it," does not mean that "it" is safe or good or secure for children. Some parents want their children to have every advantage, and any new gate to learning seems to them a guarantee of personal fulfillment and a harbinger of family honor. There are also parents who reason that, if special public care is good for the handicapped or the deprived, it must be good for their children. But this is like sending all healthy children to the hospital to be sure that they get the same benefits as the youngsters who are sick.

In part, poor communication is responsible for the present early schooling trend. For one thing, information has not been translated from the technical jargon of the researcher to the everyday language of the parent and educational planner. For another, many researchers, intent on digging up new facts, rely on other people to interrelate their data with that of different scientists and to use this information for educational planning.

For years, a number of leading specialists in early

childhood education and special education have been concerned that planners and legislators were ignoring the facts established by early childhood research. Earl Schaefer (129) of the University of North Carolina, former head of early childhood research for National Institutes of Health, says that "Although much . . . [ECE] research data has been generated during the last decade . . . they have . . . as yet had minimal impact on educational planning. . . ." Speaking more strongly, Morvin Wirtz (154) of Western Michigan University, former director of the federal Division of Education of the Handicapped and Rehabilitation, insists that ". . . many of our programs in early childhood education operate from the gut level without basis in research. Drawers are full of research evidence, but they are ignored."

We would be aghast at such a performance in medical science. We would not tolerate such ignorance even in the manufacture of our cars. Yet our gullibility seems almost without bounds when educators and legislators propose to shape our children. Whether or not these planners are well-intentioned is not the issue here. The real issue is: What is best for our children?

In view of research findings on children's needs and on the performance of preschools and care centers, more and more people are asking questions about early childhood education. Dale Meers (96), a Washington, D.C. psychoanalyst and researcher, was once an avid proponent of early schooling. But he now questions providing day care for *all* children simply because it is needed by the disadvantaged. He asks if we would give methadone, the drug cure, to all adults simply because it is needed by addicts. Other early childhood specialists are modifying or reversing their blanket endorsements of preschool. The consensus of scientific evidence on the home versus the preschool is clear for the majority of children. They receive a better foundation for future development and learning from a secure and responsive home environment in which understanding parents are the teachers. Thus, before enrolling a child in the local preschool or care center, one should ask if he will clearly be better off there than at home.

Many leading early childhood specialists now are beginning to mark out a new course. Their basic consideration is to harmoniously balance a child's faculties with his physical and emotional development. They stress that every child should be carefully screened at a very early age to determine if he has any learning handicaps, and periodic checkups should follow thereafter. For they reason that while the development of the mind is important, the body is the powerhouse for the young child's brain and central nervous system. A sound body and stable emotions provide a strong foundation for mental and social maturity. Without this soundness and stability, the child will not realize his greatest potential.

2.

Making the Laws

There is no shortage of innovation these days in ECE. Much creative progress has been made, particularly in medical and psychological screening of young children. Yet, in many cases, innovation means little more than change for the sake of change. Studies are now under way to determine why state legislatures have passed laws mandating or inducing schooling for little children down to age 6 or 5 or 4. To date, these studies have found that no systematic research was used as a basis for these laws.

Why, then, have we had the recent massive attempts to establish early schooling programs? The answer can be found partly in politics. For years, there has been a power struggle among some educators and state legislators. California (24) is a prominent example. Unfortunately for its young children, that state, in an attempt to bring back respect and authority to the Office of the State Superintendent of Schools, which some felt had been lost by the attitudes of the previous superintendent, has focused on the early schooling issue. For many years, California was one of the few states that permitted children to stay out of school until they were 8 years of age. Then, in the late 1960's, a movement was initiated that resulted in lowering the *mandatory* school age to 6 years, an age at which school entrance had been long *permitted.* Few scientific or common sense reasons were offered for this action. Some legislators noted that other states were doing it without serious parent protest, while others felt that it would get children off the streets.

In 1970, a new state school superintendent, Dr. Wilson Riles, was elected. He was dedicated to even earlier schooling. Dr. Riles (120) was convinced that readiness was an outmoded concept in education. He said there should be less attention paid to readiness and more to action. In other words, he inferred that children did not have to be ready mentally, physically or emotionally in order to go to school without risk.

Dr. Riles had already participated in statewide planning and legislation as a ranking state education officer. Among his first acts in early 1971 was the appointment of the California Task Force on Early Childhood Education. Note the sequence of developments that followed: He charged this group with preparing a plan that would make preschooling available for *all* California children on a tax-supported basis. The Task Force's final draft report (23) recommended new primary schooling between the ages of 4 and 8, with the child eligible to enter on his fourth birthday, but making enrollment voluntary until age 5. The specific implication here was that the child may eventually be required to enroll at age 5. This would extend downward yet another year the present California school law.

Then Dr. Riles's report to the California State Board

of Education in March 1972 recommended ". . . a new type of public education for all children who have attained the age of three years and nine months as of September 1." (p. iii). Because of heavy pressures from alarmed parents, administrators and researchers, these recommendations were not included in the final printed Task Force Report, nor were they passed into law. But the state's direction was on the record (120), ". . . school attendance . . . is still optional until age six. However, it is intended that at a point in time in the future an approvable program must be offered to all children who wish to attend public education at age four." And California has long been one of the pacesetters for the nation.

The published version of the California Task Force Report (24) insisted that ". . . grade level barriers between the preschool year, the kindergarten, and the present primary grades should be removed so that children may make continual progress through the primary school." For children who are ready for school, such unrestricted progress through a nongraded system suggests strong educational planning. But if taken literally, this document implies that young children from 3 years, 9 months to 8 years of age should be involved in systematic schooling in the basic skills.

While Dr. Riles doubted the children's need of readiness for formal instruction, his supporters assume that much of the early instruction would be just that—preparing the child for later academic work. The published report specified that, "All children must acquire the basic tools of learning in reading, oral and written language, and arithmetic, by the time they are ready to leave the primary school" (p. 5).

The California Task Force (24) repeatedly infers the need for flexibility and freedom in this experience. Yet in outlining these requirements, it calls for increased "intensity" in the "educational programs during the early growth period" (p. 2). We must not assume that in calling for intensity and for "formal" education, a state is demanding rigidity in its program. California leaders should be given credit for planning the best, most flexible programs that can be created in a preschool, in trying to teach the basic skills to children under 6 or 7. This is their ideal. But few, if any, such ideals are reached in mass education. At best, California state officials are calling for systematic academic experiences for preschool children. *This is precisely what young children of this age do not need.*

Many California county, city and local officials have their doubts about the state's proposals. Administrators have expressed a willingness to give the program a chance, but they found the California plan, as presented to them, virtually impossible to administer. One letter to Dr. Riles from County Superintendent Walter A. Eagan, his deputy and 16 district superintendents, called the state planning an "abomination," that ". . . has been demoralizing, discouraging and disheartening to staff members and citizens. . . ." Others told us they would have to go along if the law were passed. One high county school officer in Northern California privately put it this way, "Of course these little kids should be at home. But if we are given state or federal money for preschools, the voter will be on our necks if we don't take it. It becomes a matter of keeping your job."

Other states, from Florida to Alaska and from Hawaii to New York, are also interested in preschool education. In the early 1900's, the age in Texas for even *permitting* school entry was 8 years. This was lowered by state law to age 7 in 1907–1908. A generation later, in 1930–1931, this was dropped another year to age 6, even though the mandatory age remained at 7. (Some of the damage attributed to such lowering of entrance ages is recorded in Chapter 9.) Now in some parts of Texas, such as the city of Houston (143), provision is being made for public education as young as 3½.

Florida has taken a guarded course. In the words of one Florida early childhood leader, ". . . to provide early schooling or even day-care for all Florida's children is a very big step. We are not sure that we are ready for it yet" (2). Accordingly, Florida is making a careful study of research evidence and its possible application to Florida's needs.

Hawaiian preschool proponents pressed urgently for legislation, but were defeated in 1973. In Arizona there were widely felt pressures to lower the state's school entrance age to age 6. But, as in Hawaii, when the legislators were presented with sound research data to the contrary, they voted the measure down. In New York, where a law similar to the California bill was passed in 1967, legislators tied its implementation to the availability of money. As of 1974, the money had not yet been made available, and New York had begun to experiment with family day care, which research recommends over schools.

Sheldon White (153), Harvard psychologist, following his massive study of federal early childhood programs, has expressed disappointment in their accomplishment. He has voiced concern that the early schooling movement ". . . will work itself into so much trouble . . . that it will wipe out the gains special education has made and possibly ruin the future of childhood education."

Unfortunately, many preschool proponents still urge that universal care be provided for all children, regardless of need. Dr. Edward Zigler (160), formerly head of the U. S. Office of Child Development, warns against this point of view and suggests a likely course for future planning:

I do not think that the solution to the nation's child care problem is to provide every young child with a preschool education or to place every child from a certain age on in a child care center. I believe that we should do everything in our power to strengthen and support family life rather than supplant it in any way. We must provide good substitute socializing settings for children of mothers who choose to work. But we should be wary of those who suggest that centers or experts are intrinsically superior to home settings. We must be aware of how the nature of the family has changed. We should use this awareness in developing social institutions that are not just centers for children, but also institutions that work directly toward supporting family life.

Not long ago, psychologist Harold W. Stevenson (141), chairman of the Advisory Committee on Child Development of the National Academy of Sciences's National Research Council, promised

. . . a major attempt at taking a long-term look at our nation's child development policies and goals, . . . [and an] attempt to specify the minimal requirements for sound development of children up to eight years old, to determine how adequately various existing federal and non-federal programs are meeting these needs, and to propose new approaches where these needs are not being met.

Much is already being done in this direction. In addition to Sheldon White's major study, Cornell's Urie Bronfenbrenner (20) a well-known child and family specialist has also made a wide-ranging analysis of the directions of early childhood education. And many aspects of early childhood have been examined by professionals under the direction of Dr. Edith Grotberg, Chairman of the U.S. Government's Interagency Council on early childhood education (59) and of Dr. Sally Ryan (127) of the office of the secretary, Department of Health, Education and Welfare. Meanwhile, Yale's Edward Zigler (160), North Carolina's Earl Schaefer (129, 130), Peabody's Susan Gray (56) and Stanford's Robert Hess (69) are among those observing the outcome of early childhood research and pointing toward the home as normally the best avenue for child care.

Yet many early schooling advocates freely quote experiments and research to support their position. These have included powerful groups such as the Educational Policies Commission (38), then affiliated with both the National Education and the American Association of School Administrators, which called for publicly supported educational programs for all children, beginning with 4-year-olds. The California Task Force on Early Childhood Education (24) underscored the importance of research; but neither individually nor collectively did quoted studies support the California idea of providing preschool for *all* children.

California Superintendent Riles (120) began his charge to his early childhood task force with a statement based on Dr. Bloom's (14) questionable conclusions. The Task Force (24) even more specifically used—or misused—the Bloom inferences as its cornerstone. The final *Report of the Task Force on Early Childhood Education* (24) also cites (pp. 36, 37) the famous orphanage study by Dr. Harold Skeels (135). In this experiment 3- and 4-year-old orphans were divided into two groups. The children who remained under controlled conditions in standard orphanage care declined in mental ability and later potential. Those children in the experiment who were taken out and given special care made substantial gains and, in most cases, became productive citizens. As quoted in the *Report*, the latter children attended nursery school and kindergarten. It is therefore inferred that such schooling is good for all. This is like saying, if you can help a child by taking him off the cold street and housing him in a warm tent, then warm tents should be provided for *all* children—when obviously most children already have even more secure housing.

The gains made by the children in the experiment can hardly be credited to early schooling, or even to normal day care. Rather, the three highly important factors appear to be that each child had his own surrogate mother, or a one-to-one relationship; each was with his "mother" continuously over a long period of time and the contrasting orphanage environment was so sterile and sad that almost anything would have been an improvement. The fact that the surrogate mothers were retarded teenagers demonstrates that parents do not have to be brilliant to rear bright, happy children. The California Task Force Report quoted Dr. Susan Gray (58) as making a similar analysis of the likely reason for the children's gains, but it ignored the analysis in its conclusions. We will note in Chapter 5 how research shows that, at these early ages, the most powerful stimulus to a child's development is warm, continuous mothering.

The California Task Force also cited (pp. 39–44) eleven preschool demonstration projects over the nation as examples of what California could do. But we should note that in the great majority of these projects there was at least one adult for each five children. This should be a maximum ratio of children per adult. Yet California recommended a program starting with one adult to *ten* children. And school administrators well know how, with limited finances, they soon are pressured to take even more children per teacher. Moreover, not one of these demonstration projects is considered by the profession-at-large to have proven itself beyond doubt. Many years must elapse before the eventual results of such care can be determined. And in most cases, the care was provided for disadvantaged children—quite a different matter from providing care for normal children.

Because the *Report* cited none of the powerful research contrary to its conclusions, we questioned the validity of the California proposal in a nationwide series of articles in professional, congressional and popular journals in 1972. These, in turn, were carried by the news media, causing consternation among laymen and professionals and bringing a wide-ranging reaction. We were not surprised, for we knew that feelings ran strong in the powerful preschool and day-care movement.

We had been led by professional literature to believe that most parents and educators were moving in the direction of the California Task Force. We were astonished, however, to find that letters from our readers supported our position more than five to one. These included parents, preschool teachers, administrators and planners, university professors, researchers, legislators, and local, county and state school administrators. More often than not, there seemed to be a sense of relief that science supports the home as normally the best place for young children.

Yet popular reaction is not a safe guide. There was now reason to redouble our efforts to obtain the best information on the development of young children. We, and others as well, have systematically searched for evidence that clearly supports the idea of universal early schooling or day care. We are forced to conclude that little, if any, exists. We have also tried to find support for those who advocate early entrance into regular school. We find that they have little or no scientific backing either. Yet, in both cases, we have found overwhelming evidence to the contrary. The remaining chapters of Part I of this book detail this information. While it is not our intention to scare parents into changing their ways and their laws, the time has come for a sober look at the facts. Congresswoman Edith Green, long-time educational leader in the House of Representatives, remarked to us in a personal conversation in 1973 that knowledge without action is futile, but action without knowledge is fatal. If, as some people believe, the American child and his family have already been sentenced unfairly, then we believe it is time for their reprieve and restoration.

3.

Some Common Fears and Questions

Mothers and fathers wonder what will happen if they do not send their children to nursery school or kindergarten. Some parents fear state laws, and with good reason. Many parents fear that their children may miss important attentions only teachers can give. For some parents, their child's social development is a major concern. Others are afraid of social pressures: What will they look like if they keep their children home from school when all the others in the neighborhood are enrolled? Still others worry that if their child starts school later, he may be out of step with the crowd.

In noting that "America is currently moving toward making preschool education available for all parents who want it for their children . . . ," one of America's most respected learning psychologists raises a finger in warning. Says David Elkind (40), "It would be a tragic mistake if the development of such programs were guided by faddish concerns and parental anxieties rather than by what we know about the need of young children."

Often parents, even those who are teachers, do not trust their ability to teach their own children in the home. Many conscientious parents are concerned about the quality of care they give. They are not sure how best to communicate with their children and to keep them constructively busy. Most of these fears are paper dragons that any normal parent can conquer readily.

Without professional training, simply by being herself, a concerned, loving mother usually can do more for her normal child than a teacher can. Parents should, of course, be willing to learn new ideas. But a mother need not be a trained teacher, *nor does she need to teach in any formal way.* By using the framework of everyday home activities in a practical way, she can help her child learn as much as possible about the things around him. Part II of this book offers parents and teachers suggestions, based on research and experience, for informally teaching children at early ages.

Children are happiest when they are busy, and keeping them busy should not be a matter for concern. Much of a child's busyness will be accomplished on his own. Much of it will come from the child's questions and curiosity. The parent's goal should be to respond to the child's questions in a patient, consistent and constructive way. Forget about the pressures of achieving. Cultivate the idea of being happily child-centered, for the child is important. Take advantage of his motivation of the moment. Be happy that he is curious, and try to go along with his curiosities whenever you can.

Preschool proponents have been outrageously successful in conveying the idea that parents are not "with it" if they do not send their children to nursery school or give them some other early schooling or care. The general impression is that most families and educators agree with them. This is not necessarily so. We have found that many parents are looking for evidence that justified keeping their children at home. In a formal poll by the administrator's journal, *Nation's Schools* (107), the large majority of the nation's school administrators seriously questioned the general need for preschools—this in spite of the fact that such programs would enlarge their domains. Parents with such considerations, however, require the advice and cooperation of educational authorities as to state-school-entrance laws, and age and grade placement. In these cases, a satisfactory solution will depend on the desire of school authorities to do the right thing for the child: to work for sound legislation rather than to share with judicial authorities the enforcement of laws that have only the remotest relationship to the child's welfare.

Analysis of a recent Stanford-based study (111) suggests that state legislatures that have voted schooling for all 4-, 5-, or 6-year-olds may have based their legislation on incomplete or misinterpreted research. Yet the determinations of these lawmakers often have been absolute. The parents must enroll their children in school at 5 or 6 or else face the threat of arrest.

Now that research has been brought together from ECE areas not systematically considered heretofore (neurophysiology, cognition, parent attitudes, etc.), such legislation should be reconsidered. Some states have shown this kind of care. As a result of systematic and comprehensive evaluation of such research, generalized early schooling proposals have been modified or turned back by Arizona, Hawaii and Mississippi, and in Georgia and New Mexico the provisions were limited to handicapped children.

One of the most common fears victimizing parents is that if the young child does not have a variety of socializing experiences out of his home, he will not develop well socially. A seriously deprived child surely may require unique social stimulation. But his typical need will be for parental response, rather than for early schooling. If his parents cannot or will not respond to him firmly and lovingly, the small family type school or day care may be the answer.

A reason often given for the trend toward early schooling is that such experience gives a child opportunity to learn how to get along with others. Several questions should be raised about this presumed benefit of early schooling. What is the evidence that these children actually do get along better? What *kind* of socialization should they have? Do we want them simply to make many acquaintances? Or do we expect them to develop concern and consideration for others and respect for older people? What do we really mean by "getting along"? Are these values really best developed in a crowded situation, where a child has relatively little attention from an adult whom he can use as a pattern? Or will he find more identity of the right kind in a home where his parents can respond to him on a consistent, warm and constructive basis throughout the day, and where youngsters in the neighborhood can challenge his selfish ideas? The so-called preschool socializing process does not necessarily socialize ideally (Chapters 5 and 6).

In fact, there is considerable support for the notion that, for most children, the preschool is not the best for social purposes. The young child needs a free but somewhat protected environment. He should not be subjected to undue excitement or competition until he develops the ability to reason consistently—and until he has reached a level of maturity at which he perceives well and begins to see his environment in a less selfish perspective. Until then, he cannot see another's point of view. This applies even when he is at home, although the demands of school often induce more selfishness than generosity in the social life of the 5 or 6 year old. And such selfish attitudes generally limit his sociability.

Parents should make up their minds what kind of children they want, and what sacrifices they are willing to make. They should be aware of what they can do that teachers never can provide. They should consider carefully how much they risk when they place their children in environments over which they have little control. Children like to act "big." They want to be like "the big kids." This would be fine if they imitated the best qualities of their idols. Unfortunately, this is not so often the case. Children quickly pick up new tastes, mannerisms and speech, and too often the worst of these. This is less likely to happen if they remain in a reasonably good home until age 8 or 10.

SOME LEGITIMATE FEARS

There are a number of clearly justified areas of concern for parents. More often than not, they are cleared up by an understanding of the young child's limitations.

Few parents, for example, correctly estimate a young child's ability to communicate. They may judge correctly his ability to understand a simple order or expression of love. Yet they often fail to recognize that until a child approaches the age of reason, about 8 years of age, he may not understand correctly what they have in mind. He may not yet be able to see or hear discriminately. He may develop fears from simple games such as hide-and-seek. His ability to perceive and to judge is not yet mature.

These little misunderstandings too often are treated lightly by adults. They deserve thoughtful attention, because they may be painful or even tragic occasions for the children. They may, for example, come from a young child's normal inability to hear sounds discriminately, One small child of our acquaintance came home from Sunday school convinced that "Jesus is taking the birdies all away." The song that day was, "Jesus takes my *burdens* all away."

An ability to communicate simply, clearly, lovingly and without baby talk is one of the parents' greatest teaching tools. Here again the average parent has a real advantage over most teachers. (Chapter 8 goes more deeply into the ability of the child to reason.)

Parents sometimes fear that their children will be embarrassed if they start school as late as 8, when other children go to school at 6. Preschool planners also occasionally deride the idea of late school entrance. They, like some parents, assume that such children will graduate from high school at 20 or 21. They not only fear that the children will be too old for their grades, but warn that they may become misfits.

They are right if they make the 8-year-old begin at the first grade and lumber lock step through all eight grades. But this should not be. A child who stays out an extra year or two before enrolling in a typical school should be allowed to start at least a grade or two later. He will usually catch up with his peers in a few weeks or months, and will often pass them.

This practice seldom, if ever, creates serious problems, if administrators and teachers are open-minded and cooperate with the parents. Out of about 400 late entrants on our records, only four reported difficulty. In each case, they were children who were required by parent or teacher to start in the first grade at age 8 or 9. They were either physically too large or were social misfits at the first grade level.

A nongraded school of course is the idea. It is a sound,

logical, old-fashioned idea that recalls the best of the one-room rural school. It has, in recent years, returned to favor among many parents and educators. Expressed in its simplest way, it provides flexibility for the child to proceed at his own academic speed within his range of social and emotional maturity.

In any event, the 8-year-old should be allowed to advance quickly to his social group. Given normal practical experiences around the home, he will be well along on readiness for his later reading and arithmetic chores. And what he doesn't have, he soon will get. The child who is treated sensibly in this way will usually catch up and pass the other children in achievement and all-around development. He is also much less likely to be a discipline problem. Any well-informed teacher or school administrator will understand these principles.

Still another common fear of parents is having to meet state laws that are encouraging or requiring earlier and earlier school enrollment. In many communities, school authorities agree to permit later enrollment if the child is provided a sound home environment. Others cling rigidly to the letter of the law, fearing that, if they do not, there will be a loss in financial aid to the school district, since most schools are financed on the basis of average daily attendance.

Recently, a number of mothers, profoundly aware of their children's home needs, have faced criminal indictment rather than turn their children over to the schools too soon. The school districts involved range from Marquette and Detroit, Michigan, to Napa County, California. Yet, usually, district attorneys and judges have thrown out the indictments without trial when they have looked over the research evidence about early schooling.

Sound educators are more concerned about the welfare of the children in their care than they are about the jot and title of the law. They work for the best possible environment for the child. When they are caught in the grip of an unreasonable law, they try to see that the law is taken to court. There is sufficient evidence from sound educational research to challenge the validity of school laws that *require* children to be in school before age 8, unless the home environment is intolerable. There is sufficient legal precedent, provided by the Amish and others, to give parents courage to question these laws. And there is no basis in common sense for laws that call children to school before they are ready.

SOME COMMON QUESTIONS

Some parents' questions are more practical than fearful. The answers to many of these are found in later chapters of this book. But several require more direct responses at this point.

We commonly hear, "What is wrong with sending a child to nursery school for two or three hours daily, several days a week?" We must answer that in general not even the "best" schools compare favorably with a good home. Recently, we asked the leading teacher of one of Paris' finest preschools how she would compare the responsive care she was able to give her preschoolers with the care they could have in the home. Her response was an emotional wish: "Oh, if I could only have them two or three at a time in my apartment!" And there are other factors to consider:

1. Any school situation at these early ages is at best a substitute for the home. Gesell Institute's psychologist Louise Ames (5) points out that the home provides a "three dimensional" experience of real living, while school tends to be a "two dimensional" alternative. This comparison which Dr. Ames applies to primary schools is

even more valid during the preschool years.

2. Some children sense their placement in preschool or day care as parental rejection. And in many cases they are right. Parents often place their personal freedom before the child's welfare.

3. In a preschool an intimate relationship with an adult is virtually impossible for every child, especially in terms of the loving personal responses every small child needs.

4. Separation from parents at this age usually causes a degree of insecurity to all children, some more than others, even though it may not be obvious to the parent or teacher. In some cases this separation lays the base for severe emotional and learning problems later on.

5. In sending them away from home, parents subject their children to influences that they cannot control, not only as far as the teacher is concerned, but also with regard to the collective and individual influences of other children. Since the children are unable to reason consistently, they are often confused by mores and values in the home that conflict with those in school. Children in preschool centers frequently tend to accept other adults and other environments in place of the parent and the home, and gradually ignore or reject parents. It is not unusual for them to place the word of their teachers ahead of their own parents.

6. A few nursery schools are excellent, and many schools are outstandingly staffed. Yet many others are not good nor well staffed, and public supervision of these schools is seldom adequate. Fluctuations of personnel because of illness, vacations, and other circumstances have been found to be traumatic to a child who has established an attachment to the teacher or aide who is absent.

7. Children sometimes find out that preschool is more "dessert" than "vegetables." Certain freedoms not possi-

ble at home, the abundance of toys and equipment and the absence of chores may make them resentful of home restrictions before they are able to understand the reasons for the differences.

8. Mothers and fathers, noting the apparent anticipation in their youngsters when they first trot off to school, fail to see that their excitement sometimes may be a symptom of anxiety. It may also signal the children's desire for a change from home or because "the other kids are doing it." Unfortunately, these experiences often bring frustration or disillusionment simply because the children are not mature enough for school.

9. At a time when every effort should be made to keep a child's life quiet, simple and uncluttered, preschool often complicates his life with hurrying, daily transportation, and overstimulation of a group when he is not mature enough to cope with more than a few children at a time.

10. Competition with a number of his peers for toys and space, and in physical or mental abilities usually is a strain on young children. Family life for the first 8 years tends to prepare a child more gently for the competition he must eventually face.

11. Once a child enrolls in school he usually becomes locked into institutional life for the remainder of his childhood years, and desirable family freedoms are gone. Whether or not the parents see this as a sacrifice, it usually turns out to be so for the child.

12. There is no systematic evidence from research that supports the need for nursery schooling for the child who has a good home.

13. Parents often use the preschool as a crutch—passing to the preschool certain childhood problems they cannot handle or behavior they cannot understand.

In our society, it is the parents, not the preschool

teachers, who are accountable for their children's behavior. Furthermore, parents are often frustrated by their children, because of their own failures in rearing them. These parents frequently fail to think of their children as individuals in the home, with their own privileges and responsibilities. They grant privileges to the children but do not help them learn responsibility, order, industry, honesty and similar values. When they can no longer control their children, many parents punish them, in effect, by sending them away to school instead of enjoying them and working daily with them to build their values.

Another common question is: Don't you think children need some freedom from their homes? We have already noted that the kind of freedom children need is not normally *from* home, but to work out their fantasies *in* a home. Yet some children do need freedom from their homes, when their homes are physically or emotionally disastrous. This, however, is no reason for concluding that preschool programs bring freedom and should be provided for all children. Try to look at your preschool through the eyes of your child. If you see more freedom for him there than in your home, something is wrong within your home. A good home provides far more freedom than a preschool. There are exceptions, but normally, as soon as children are placed together in group care, the operation tends to become standardized. The child generally has to adjust to the norm, which almost always interferes with his legitimate freedom. The brighter he is, the more he feels the restrictions. Yet, by the nature of this kind of care, rules must be applied that curtail a number of his normal liberties. Few adults appreciate the terror behind a quiet whimper, or the patent loneliness or fear under the cloak of childish rebellion. Group discipline may be more nearly appropriate when the child has achieved a balance in his maturity, at about 8–10 years of age. (See Chapter 4, on the IML.)

Another common question is: Have you ever tried living with a small child in an apartment day in and day out? The answer is, "Yes." And certainly a city apartment may not be the best place to rear a child, much less a small corner in a tenement. Yet imaginative use of nearby parks, zoos, museums, stores, pet shops, and even water-fronts, add up to a climate superior to many city schools and care centers.

Despite these possibilities, there are many situations that are intolerable for the young child. Some parents cannot or will not be helped to provide reasonable care. These circumstances demand an alternate to the home. And for these children, the public purse should be opened to provide the nearest thing to a sound home. Wise, wonderful and affectionate preschool teachers who sacrifice daily to be surrogate mothers or fathers are true friends of disadvantaged children. Not all preschool-age children, disadvantaged or not, are so lucky. However sympathetic we may be with the plight of parents who are forced to relinquish the upbringing of their children, on the basis of research and clinical observation, it is still evident that, in most cases, the child is making the greater sacrifice.

4.

When They Are Ready for School

Of real consequence is the parents' concern that they may not know enough about the developmental needs of their children to be totally responsible for them for the first eight years. We suggest that if parents can, they should interview elementary school teachers, particularly a special reading teacher, about the characteristics, attitudes, problems and motivational differences of their pupils in the first four grades.

From a good teacher, parents will learn that some children who develop school difficulties will be emotionally unstable or immature. Others will have vision or hearing problems. Still others started school too soon, and within two or three years, lost the early excitement of school and the motivation to achieve; their minds were simply not ready to reason out their lessons. In each case, a maturity level has not been reached. The child's performance has been thrown out of balance. He is like a person with one leg shorter than another. No matter how hard he tries to run gracefully and fast, he will be unable to compete with one who is normal.

If the children start school later, their teachers will tell you they normally will not become frustrated by their regular school tasks. They will perform easily and readily and are less likely to lose their first excitement of learning. They had an advantage over the early entrants who were handicapped because they had not developed a harmonious maturity. Chapter 9, on early and late starters, provides some background research data for this subject.

Teachers have long understood the practical consequences of balanced maturity—or the lack of it. They call it readiness. It has been a loosely defined term, but of immense significance. Unfortunately, because of its omnibus characteristics and its lack of definition, the concept of readiness has often been overlooked, bypassed or deliberately ignored by educational planners. This inattention to readiness may also explain, in part, why so many legislators in so many states have worked to get children into school earlier and earlier.

A further explanation has to do with our tendency to narrow our view of things. Scientists often tend by the very nature of their work to restrict themselves to small parts of a total field. As they concentrate on their own areas, they sometimes fail to relate their work to the research of others outside their fields. Neurophysiologists, for example, work with the brain and nervous system, optometrists and ophthalmologists study the eyes, the cognitive psychologists spend most of their time on learning problems and sociologists and psychiatrists are occupied with the relationships and environments of people. Yet, as a general principle, any scientific study is usually of greater value when joined with research from related areas. When even one or two of these investigators cross-fertilize their findings with those made in other fields, a great deal of good is often produced. And when the knowledge and research of *all* these people are brought together, new directions and major developments can take shape. This is particularly true of early childhood education, where the integration of research has produced a new profile of the child's needs. Thus professional child development people and state legislators both have a vested interest in insisting that research findings be brought together systematically.

Early childhood education must take into account the development of the child's brain, vision, hearing, perception, emotions sociability, family and school relationships and physical growth. For each of these factors, there appears to be a level of maturity at which most children can, without serious risk, leave normal homes and begin typical school tasks. When we bring these factors together, we have an index to total maturity that we call the child's integrated maturity level (IML).* This level may be as

---

*While the maturity level idea is hardly new, the concept of integration in the sense described above is stated here for the first time in an early childhood book. So a definition and technical explanation is given for the early childhood scholar.

The integrated maturity level is the point at which the developmental variables (affective, psychomotor, perceptual and cognitive) within the child reach an optimum peak of readiness in maturation and cooperative functioning for out-of-home group learning (typical school) experiences.

The IML implies an integration, or cooperative functioning, of the various aspects of human development in a level or degree of coordination that becomes more productive as maturation progresses.

Aspects of human development, or the variables within the person, include the affective, psychomotor, perceptual and cognitive behaviors. As maturation progresses, the degree of coordination among these variables is indicated by a higher level of motivation and an increased ability to learn without undue stress and strain. When all the variables have matured to the point that optimum integration of function is possible, an appropriate state of readiness has been reached for structured school learning experiences.

important a guide to readiness for school as the IQ is to school counseling and may offer a clear and impressive planning base for parents and teachers. On the basis of a comprehensive review of many research findings outlined in the following chapters, we believe that the IML is seldom, if ever, achieved earlier than ages 8–10.

When we found that neurophysiologists and learning psychologists arrived independently at the same ages—about 8–10—for the beginning of school tasks, we began systematically to review studies of the brain and of perception. Our attention was also directed to related research areas, such as vision and hearing. In fact, we found that a number of areas had been largely ignored by many educational planners. The results of this ignorance are common and serious misconceptions and lack of information in the field of early childhood education. Misconceptions and misinformation are common on the importance of mothering, on comparisons of early and late school entrants and on parental attitudes. In each case, we found that the consensus of research clearly supported the brain specialists and the psychologists.

With regard to vision, hearing and, to some extent, maternal deprivation, we were astonished to find that maturity levels coincided remarkably with the 8–10–year-old findings. And careful search yielded little contrary evidence. These findings are especially surprising in light of the state and national trend toward earlier and earlier schooling for all children.

We do not say that the authorities agree on all details. It is obvious that much research remains to be done in all areas of early childhood. However, all available knowledge about the growth and development of children at these ages should be brought together, and each child's IML determined. Only then can we know how to provide children the help they need most.

5.

Developing Attachments

From birth, a child relates to his world as he learns about it; and he learns about it as it, in turn, responds to him. He learns with sureness and accuracy or with a hazy confusion, depending upon the people and things around him. He learns from warmth, consistency and love, and opens as a flower in the sunshine to whatever new experience or knowledge may come his way. Or he learns from coldness, irritability and neglect, and closes his mind and feelings against further hurt. He rejects those who already have rejected him.

Personal success for the child, including his later achievement and adjustment in school, depends to a large degree upon a stable, predictable, consistent early environment. A child needs a secure base from which to explore. He becomes self-reliant as he realizes that he can rely on others, and that the important people and basic things in his world are not always changing. This is why the child should not suddenly be left in group situations. He should be allowed to become acquainted with new people and places gradually, while maintaining a consistent, sound basic attachment at home. Yet early schooling proponents suggest taking the normal child from his natural and most secure habitat, the home, at the critical period of between 3 and 8 years of age, and requiring him to establish a whole new set of relations.

The small child needs to be with those to whom he best relates. In most cases, this will be his parents. Parents who do not relate well to their children should be helped to understand how to do so. The development of a warm, wholesome parent-child relationship should be one of the principal objectives of a sound parent-education program. In fact Burton White (152), the head of Harvard's early childhood center, emphasizes the urgent need for parent education, particularly for young adults, to help them guide the educational development of their children during the first years of life. If parents can be helped to become more effective, thereby making a lasting contribution to their own children, they will bring large benefits to society. Confident parents are in a position to help their children become thinkers as well as learners. Such children can become more constructive members of society.

This warm, responsible relationship on a consistent basis is the best foundation a young child can have not only for later schooling, but also for social development. Otherwise, concludes England's John Bowlby (18), world authority on maternal attachment and deprivation, on the basis of studies by S. Van Theis (144), they ". . . grow up to become parents deficient in the capacity to care for their children, and . . . adults deficient in this capacity are commonly those who suffered deprivation in childhood."

A vicious cycle is induced by factors that dilute or disrupt a normal home life. And one of these factors is unnecessary separation from home and family during the child's early years.

Parents who love their children, who understand their developmental needs, will note that neither research nor common sense dictates sending children away from home in their early years. University of Michigan child psychiatrist Humberto Nagera (106) declares that ". . . no other animal species will subject their infants to experiences they are not endowed to cope with except the human animal." We would not force a flower to bloom before it is ready unless we were prepared to ask for less fragrance or to watch it wither away before its time. We should have conclusive evidence before we challenge nature's normal course. And in this case, such evidence simply does not exist. In most cases, as we have said, parents provide the best social and emotional growth a child can have. The young child needs more to be happily integrated into one family, and warmly responded to, than he needs to be taught. This, of course, does not mean that parents do not teach a child anything. Parents constantly teach by precept and example. Rather, it means that the young child does not require *academic* teaching—the typical skills of reading and arithmetic. By far, most teaching in early childhood is better done by understanding the child than by building academic skills.

If the child works and plays and lives warmly and freely with his parents (or parent substitutes), in a one-to-one relationship in the home, he also has a better chance to develop sound character traits systematically: neatness, order, promptness, dependability, honesty, industry and the graces of kindness and concern for others. These lead to a positive concept of himself. Such a self-concept is the foundation for self-confidence and self-control. Such self-respect and self-control, in turn, are the finest bases for unselfish sociability and self-discipline. Then when this child goes to school, preferably at age 8 or later, he is equal to most situations. Social problems seldom threaten him. This quality of sociability is more difficult to build into the child who starts school too early.

While children do need opportunities to develop as individuals, they also seek to imitate the people who are important to them. Their models are usually parents, relatives, and later, teachers and other friends. It is strange but true that some parents would rather have their children choose models other than themselves. A surprising number of parents have poor self-concepts. So they send their children off to a preschool teacher or day-care person who has no such guilt complex if the child is not perfect.

Many mothers have feelings of inadequacy. Some of them do not even welcome their babies at birth. They may demonstrate fear, disappointment, jealousy or discouragement instead of the normal expectations of love, joy and pride. Fortunately, most of these mothers eventually accept their children. But some never do. And if they feel inadequate to meet their children's needs, they often become hostile. Relatively little data on fathers is available, and research is badly needed. But psychologists' case histories and court records are also replete with cases of children rejected or abused by their fathers.

For these reasons, pediatricians also strongly emphasize the importance of parental education both before and after the birth of the child. There is much more to be gained by having professionals help parents develop a sense of adequacy with their children than by placing children in environments that substitute for the parents and home.

Harvard psychologist Jerome Kagan (81) emphasizes

the importance of parental response in developing competence in the young child. Describing how parents sometimes condition their children to failure, he notes several commonly observed differences between the family life of the typically poor or deprived child and that of the privileged child:

First, Kagan found that poverty-ridden mothers do not talk with their children as often or as interestingly as do middle-class mothers.

Second, the middle-class mother usually provides more surprises in terms of daily conversation, facial expression and play.

Third, the middle-class mother and child in America more often enjoy a closer attachment; the mother molds the child with greater confidence, and the child responds.

Fourth, the poverty-ridden mother tends to be impulsive, and her child tends to imitate her; and with this instability and uncertainty he often becomes inhibited.

Fifth, the middle-class child is often more appreciated and applauded and tends to have a longer attention span, spending more time with a given toy and in solving problems.

Sixth, the poor child is not so highly motivated because he does not feel friendly to the caregiver or teacher. He does not emulate her nor does he care for her praise, partly because he does not admire her ideas of success. Rather, he expects failure, so he does not try to succeed.

Seventh, for the deprived child, failure tends to be less humiliating because he has not expected to succeed anyway and has not been taught to value learning skills. (Obviously these findings of Kagan's do not apply to all children of poor families. There are many studies that have found that poverty can breed responsibility and self-reliance as children share responsibilities in the home, or fend for themselves. By the same token, the indulged children of rich or middle-class families may suffer the same anxieties and frustrations and sense of failure as those of poor families. Many are not permitted or required to accept their share of family responsibilities.)

Any program, then, that builds better parental attitudes and greater understanding toward children must be considered at least a partial success. This, in fact, may be considered one of the principal accomplishments of Head Start, the government program dedicated to insuring the sound development of deprived children. While its skills programs may not have achieved what many had hoped, Head Start has accomplished much in the area of helping parents to feel more important as parents. One Head Start mother has been quoted (79) as saying, "I've learned that kids are individuals. Before I just raised them, clothed and fed them. Now I'm aware of even little differences and praise them and give them credit for what they can do at their own speed. I feel therefore I'm a better parent, and an important person. Before, I felt that anyone could do this job."

John Bowlby (18) suggests that the quality of the care that parents provide a child in his earliest years will predict his future mental health. He notes that the young child should experience a warm, intimate and continuous relationship with his mother (or permanent mother-substitute) in which both find satisfaction and enjoyment. When the child does not have this relationship, he is said to be maternally deprived.

Dr. Bowlby goes on to describe how ". . . partial deprivation brings in its train acute anxiety, excessive need for love, powerful feelings of revenge, and arising from these last, guilt and depression." He sees these problems as symptoms of neurosis and instability of character. And he adds that ". . . children aged five to eight who are already prone to emotional troubles, can easily be made far worse by a separation experience, whereas secure children of the same age may come through almost unscathed."

Many day-care and preschool enthusiasts doubt the negative effects of maternal deprivation on the progress of the child. They frequently have stated that the scientific evidence is outdated. The subject requires further study, but the findings of eminent psychiatrists and psychologists [psychiatrist John Bowlby of London's Tavistock Clinic, and psychologists René Spitz of the University of Colorado, L. J. Yarrow of the National Institute of Child Health at Bethesda, Maryland, and Mary Ainsworth of Johns Hopkins University] strongly indicate that a child's attachment to his parents is a key factor throughout his entire development.

Mary Ainsworth (1) reviews the child's needs with reference to *sufficiency* of interaction with the mother, the *quality* of the interaction and the *continuity* of the interaction. When the character of any of these is lowered or the continuity broken, the child must be considered deprived.

Social workers and judges often have observed that birds and animals seem to have a greater instinctive concern for their offspring than many human beings have for their children. The mature bird or animal will give its life, if necessary, for its defenseless young. Yet animals are incapable of the creative abilities of a human mother. A human mother or father not only has great natural instincts, but also can reason and plan responsibly for the children's future.

Children, in turn, sense their dependence upon their parents at a very early age. It is no wonder that, in the words of day-care specialist Allan S. Berger (11), ". . . the principal sources of anxiety in early childhood are: the loss of parents or separation from parents." Dr. Berger adds that this is possibly the most primitive form of anxiety. At a later stage in a child's life, his fear of losing a parent's love may be more obvious. Thus a parent should be all the more discerning of a young child's needs and should stay nearby without smothering him with affection.

Psychologists and psychiatrists agree that any child, poor or rich, may suffer deprivation. If so, he will probably develop social or psychological problems. Unfortunately, the symptoms are not always easily identified. Furthermore, when problems are noted, they may not be attributed correctly to a lack of continuous, consistent and responsive parenting. When a young child is taken from his mother or father for even a short period of time before he has thoroughly established an ability to reason things out, he may feel threatened. When he is taken from the one-to-one relationship at home with his mother and placed in group care, where he must compete for the attention of an adult, he is, to some extent, depersonalized. Bowlby (18) concluded as late as 1972 and 1973, on the basis of clinical experience, that children may suffer deprivation from such an experience until 8 or 10 years of age.

Of course, there are no perfect homes or perfect mothers. But neither are there perfect schools or perfect teachers. And there are clear indications that a concerned, loving mother who is willing to learn can usually do more for her child than can any stranger, regardless of training and ability. Psychologist Glen Nimnicht (73) suggests that parent involvement with children is vital even when the time for such activity is limited. So wise working mothers and fathers in particular will see that no unnecessary distractions interrupt their time with their children.

Nimnicht, who was formerly a principal psychologist for Head Start, was initially a strong proponent of early schooling. However, after experimenting with the early education of children in Head Start, he concluded, "There is no evidence that a young child needs to go to nursery school. It's my hunch that twenty minutes a day playing with his mother does a preschooler as much good as three hours in a classroom." Nimnicht came to this conclusion after finding that children made significant gains over brief periods when their parents played with them.

In certain respects, even the Skeels's (135) orphanage experiment simulated a home setting with a great deal of affection and many wholesome, interesting experiences geared to the children's development in their early years. While the orphans spent some hours in a kindergarten, the unique experience that contributed to their positive developmental gains was the warm, one-to-one relationship with their retarded caretakers. Kagan and Whitten (83) say a "close and persistent relationship" with adults is needed. It is not possible in most schools or out-of-home care to provide this quality of relationship between adult and child.

In Uganda, Marcelle Geber (48) tested more than 300 babies. These babies were from poor, tribal-oriented families in which the mothers were child-centered, continually caressing, cuddling and talking to their little ones. She measured the infants by standardized American tests from the Gesell Institute. *They were found to be superior to Western children, not only in emotional security, but also in physiological maturity, coordination, adaptability, sociability and language skills.*

When we first read of Dr. Geber's study, we rationalized that children reared in tropical areas often mature earlier than Westerners. But she also sampled babies from Ugandan families that were less primitive and enjoyed better incomes. Here she found that, in general, the infants received less intimate attention from their mothers.

These babies were much less mature in the above-mentioned qualities than those from the poor families, and were generally below Western norms.

Silvia Bell (10) of John Hopkins University made studies of middle-income white families and, later, of relatively low-income black families. In both studies, Dr. Bell came to the conclusion that the closer and better the quality of the mother-child relationship was, the greater the ability of the child was to learn.

Often, however, it may be necessary for a small child to relate to the adult world through a teacher. It has been found that when a mother is forced to work when she would prefer to be at home with her children, the children sense her concern for them and respond to her feelings. Even if they have to leave home for the day-care center, they expectantly await her return from work. Such a mother has a stronger, more constructive influence upon her youngsters than the mother who remains at home but would rather be someplace else. When preschool is necessary, the teacher must be careful to preserve the child's identity with his family. It is easy for teachers to enjoy their attachments with children in a way that consciously or subconsciously alienates them from their parents. Moreover, the younger the child is and the longer the time is that he spends with such a teacher, the greater is the potential damage to the child—unless the teacher clearly provides more security and a more wholesome value system than the family. The selfless and effective teacher will consider this matter of personal attachment a sacred thing. Like any good guidance specialist, she will be more concerned about bringing a sense of direction and balance to a child than to attach his personal loyalty to her.

In the 1972 Senate Hearings on Head Start and Child Development, the Senate Subcommittee staff changed the original provision of the legislation for day care from eight children per adult to four or five. In doing this, they not only acknowledged research evidence, but tacitly admitted the danger of the depersonalization process. Young children need to feel that the adults in their lives can be depended upon and are readily accessible whenever needed. This is difficult when one adult is responsible for too many children at once.

In visiting the countries of Western Europe which have long provided group care for children, we found that adult-child ratios often jump to 20, 30, or 40 or more children per adult. We found this to be particularly true in France as late as 1973. In August 1967, when Dr. Meers interviewed the director of the Hungarian Bureau of Child Care (96), the director apologized that group child care in Hungary was done strictly as an economic necessity. Every able adult had to work in order to support the economy. But she assured Dr. Meers that it was the intention of the Hungarian government to limit day care as soon as possible. She could not understand why the United States, the richest of nations, would wish to inflict on itself something that Hungary, one of the poorest countries in Europe, was trying to rid itself.

Meers also found that Czechoslovakia had become concerned enough about the distress of its young children in day care to adopt a policy similar to the one suggested by the Hungarian director. In fact, Czechoslovakian television was actively dissuading its citizens from further placements of young children in preschool or day care. From his own observations, Meers (96) graphically states the reasons for this action:

> In my own study and observations of Communist centers, I was singularly depressed by what I saw, so much so that it seemed inane to continue to photograph room after

room, center after center of passive and despondent youngsters. In speaking with staff about the age at which different children entered particular daycare centers, it seemed to me that one could visually discern direct relationship between the passivity and the length of time the children had been enrolled.

Some preschool enthusiasts are quick to disparage such examples. They say that model American preschools provide a maximum of freedom and learning opportunity. But what is maximum for even a good school hardly compares with a sound home. Children may not be passive and despondent; but, all too often, they do not feel secure, and put up with schooling only because they have no choice.

American preschool and day-care enthusiasts have also assumed the success of the kibbutzim of Israel. But by and large, their assumptions are not valid. For one thing, preschool care is neither as comprehensive nor as unanimously well received in the kibbutzim as is commonly thought. For another, there is no typical kibbutz program. While some kibbutzim provide virtually full-time child care, others are far more parent-oriented. In some kibbutzim, parents have moved away from intensive group child care and have added rooms to their homes in order to provide a closer relationship and more freedom for their children. (Some further reasons are given for this in the next chapter.)

Still other preschool proponents point to the success of the British schools. And truly, preschools in England offer a distinctive plan. In general, the child has the same teacher for at least three or four consecutive years. Children come to school late in the morning for an hour or two; and, after several hours at home, return to school for another hour or so in the afternoon. Yet even this casual approach to preschooling, with its fine continuity, still has not been proven to be a sound substitute for a good home.

While there are excellent centers that supply care that deprived children badly need, to attempt to provide this superior care for all children must be described as presumptuous. Dr. Ernest Van den Haag (147), professor of social philosophy at New York University, admits to some measure of success that extraordinary people have in certain day-care centers. "But," he says, "we cannot hope to staff the proposed institutions with extraordinary people. On the contrary, chances are that the positions to be staffed—low in income and prestige—will attract indifferent people." When this is combined with the limitations of adult-child ratios in the school group, even the fair-to-good home becomes an attractive alternative.

Many families have noted marked changes in their children when the nature of their employment has required them to make frequent moves. And the younger the age at which these adjustments or accommodations are demanded, the greater is the impact upon the child. For the preschool child, this means a double problem: adjustment from home to home and from school to school. Since the results of such accommodation cannot always be immediately seen in the child, some educators blindly believe there are no grounds for opposing situations that create these problems. But Dr. Meers (96) notes that this is much like reasoning that we should not worry about the results of thalidomide until we have witnessed a parade of children it has crippled.

In addition, psychiatrists and psychologists generally agree, on the basis of both research and clinical experience, that if a young child is forced to make an excessive number of adjustments, he is more likely to develop psychological problems. Children are creatures of simplicity and routine. Care from a variety of adults is confusing and creates anxiety. This may not be obvious to the typical parent or teacher, but the pain or anxiety is there nevertheless. Young children need a continuous one-to-one relationship with an adult or adults until they have reached the integrated maturity level at about age 8.

In normal school situations, teachers generally feel that they must be impartial, that they must treat all children alike, socially and emotionally. And this is as it should be *after* the integrated maturity level has been reached, when children have developed self-reliance and the ability to reason things out for themselves. However such impartiality is not always good for the very young child. He must have someone to whom he belongs and who belongs to him. He may often appear to be caught up in the spirit of the schoolroom. Yet he seldom enjoys merely being one in a class full of children who all belong to the teacher. In this respect, a desirable home situation comes far closer than the school to meeting the child's needs.

It should also be noted that the one who provides care in a preschool or day-care center is normally an employee. He can claim rights and privileges that most parents cannot demand. He can leave his children to aides or substitutes, or quit his job completely if he chooses. In many public care centers and preschools, the child must adjust not only to the head teacher but also to the aide and to the substitute when one of the regular staff is absent. Every such experience requiring adjustment is a potential source of anxiety in the young child's life.

These points make more understandable psychiatrist Bowlby's (18) finding that: "It must never be forgotten that even the bad parent who neglects her child is none the less providing much for him. Except in the worst cases, she is giving him food and shelter, comforting him in distress, teaching him simple skills, and above all is providing him with that continuity of human care on which his sense of security rests." Dr. Bowlby points out that the child may be ill-fed and ill-sheltered, dirty and even suffering from disease; sometimes he may even be ill-treated. "But unless his parents have wholly rejected him, he is secure in the knowledge that there is *someone* to whom he is of value. . . ." and who will take care of him, at least to some degree, until he can fend for himself. It is against this background that Dr. Bowlby concludes on the basis of studies by Simonson, Theis and others, and from clinical experience that children thrive better in bad homes than in good institutions.

Preschool advocates believe that it is the very young child, from about birth to age 2 or 3, who is the most greatly damaged by separation from his parents. This is true. Yet, according to a study by Bowlby (18), although a child's vulnerability to parental separation is diminishing, it is still present until age 5. "After the age of five vulnerability diminishes still further, though there can be no reasonable doubt that a fair proportion of children between the ages of five and seven or eight are unable to adjust satisfactorily to separations." In a statement some 20 years later, Bowlby (16) confirms his conviction that many children are vulnerable to maternal deprivation to as late as 10 years of age. He feels that:

> The criticizing of parents and taking the children out of the home and putting them into the schools as is being commonly suggested these days actually undermines the parental confidence in the parent's own role, and in their potential role. There is entirely too much criticism. Some educators are guilty of undermining the home rather than building it up.

As a child grows, his attachments ideally will broaden to include brothers, sisters, relatives and neighborhood children. But normally, the mother is still the child's central attachment figure, on whom he relies while he builds self-confidence, and from whom he gradually extends his attachments without being thrust into a sink-or-swim situation. Wherever possible the father, of course, should share this privilege and responsibility.

6.

Opportunity for Parents

In principle, a young child, given reasonable freedom and personal guidance, develops better outside the classroom than within it. This is particularly true of the first 8 years or so. M. W. Sullivan, one of the earliest educational programmers, is quoted by George B. Leonard (89) on the availability of such freedom even in the city. Sullivan was asked how a child could develop socially out of school and how he would ever learn to get along with other kids. He, in turn, asked for proof that the school does a better socializing job than the home. Then he added:

> In my own case, I was the only kid in my neighborhood who was sent to kindergarten. It was optional then in Connecticut. So for almost a year my peer group was out playing, learning, creating their own very exciting world while I

was being tortured in school. They built a treehouse. They built a hut. And what did I do? I learned how to lie on a mat, how to listen to stories, how to line up, how to sit still. Finally, I figured how to escape. I wet my pants and they sent me home. They sent me home. The first time was an accident, but after that I made sure to do it every day. And I was free to learn again (p. 104).

Too many parents and teachers, as we noted before, are overconcerned about the social development of the young child. They assume that social development gives a child an ability to hold his own without fear in the midst of a group of people. But children who appear sociable and seem able to get around well with their peers are not necessarily well socialized. To be truly sociable means to have a concern for others, to know how to practice the golden rule and be willing to serve. Yet the idea of treating others as they would like to be treated is far from the minds and behavior of many young children who are supposed to have been socialized by preschool. Concerned parents can best instruct their children themselves—or by their own example.

Temple University psychologist Laurel Tanner (143) points out that the socialization of the child requires giving or giving up something. Parents should provide opportunities for their children to help others, even to the point of their child giving up a cherished toy or a bit of play time. Among the things the child may have to give up, adds Dr. Tanner, is the right to do what he feels like doing at a given moment. Furthermore, she notes that giving up should be reinforced through immediate recognition of the good to others as well as to the child himself. And she suggests that such activities be carried on throughout the child's early life.

Seldom mentioned in early childhood literature is the small child's need for freedom to be by himself, just to *be* himself. Yet one of the young child's greatest needs is for solitude. He must have time alone to work out and act out his fantasies. To him, a stick in a sandbox may be a person. A flower may be something that talks. The wind may be a friend or a dreaded enemy. And all kinds of figures legitimately play in his mind. In general, distraction is something he needs least during these years. Let him alone to play out his visions and his dreams. Let him run his own world some of the time—in the mud or the sand-pile, with a pet, if he has one, or just bossing his toys around. His need to be alone is certainly as great, and sometimes greater, than his need to be socialized, especially in a school setting. Arnold Gesell, the late dean of early childhood specialists, admonished parents:

> Lead your child out into nature. Teach him on the hilltops and in the valleys; there he will listen better. But in these hours of freedom let him be taught by nature rather than by you. Let him fully realize that she is the real teacher, and that you with your art do nothing more than to walk quietly by her side. Should a bird sing, or an insect hum on a leaf, at once stop your talk. Birds and insects are teaching him. You may be silent.

Dr. Gesell was concerned that education ". . . is too often confounded with verbal instruction and recitation and word drill." He felt that ". . . the deepest and most educative experiences are wordless contact with things."

We were poignantly reminded of this need for alone-ness in a recent interview with the head of a seminar for Israeli kibbutz teachers. With great insight, she pointed out some facts not commonly realized about group influ-ences:

A lot of the children who grew up in the kibbutz say that they had no chance for solitude when they were children. Everything was always group, group, and that was always stressed for them. They couldn't even sit around alone and cry in their rooms alone if they wanted to, because there was always somebody else in the room. And they were always encouraged to do everything in groups. And when you do things in groups, there's always a pecking order just as with dogs, cats, and even horses in a corral.

And there is always a scapegoat. And once you become a scapegoat in the group in the children's home, you're also the scapegoat of the group in school, because you go to school with the children you live with. There's no chance of escape.

To the perceptive child psychologist, who has worked with groups of young children, such pictures are not new. Group therapy may be good for adults, but it is not usually best for little children. For them, one person and one thing at a time is a good rule for most of the day. They need time to learn to relate to a few people who are important to them—usually their family or those with whom they live.

Wherever possible, children should be given time to build a solid base in a relatively quiet, uncluttered and predictable environment. This unhurried security makes possible a great deal of basic learning, most of it achieved quite unconsciously. Martin Engel (43), formerly head of the Health, Education and Welfare National Demonstration Center in Early Childhood Education, notes that ". . . kids learn from parents and teachers very little of what is intentionally, consciously taught. What kids do in fact learn is modeled upon what we are, not what we preach; not what we say, but how we say it; not what we ask of children, but what we ourselves do." The more parents come to understand this basic learning process, the less likely they will be to delegate it to someone over whom they themselves have little control. And the brighter the child, the greater will be his need for solitude and for an uncluttered environment, guided but free, so that he may shape the foundation for his world.

Probably the greatest single goal of early childhood education should be to build in children a sense of their own worth as persons. The child must learn to feel that he is needed and valued by those about him. This is one of the richest gifts his parents can give. His value system is built best through sharing family responsibilities from his earliest years. As the child senses that he is a cog in the family machine, and that the family organization runs more smoothly with his help, he gradually develops stability both in terms of businesslike behavior and thoughtfulness toward others. He realizes that people can count on him, and with this knowledge he normally gains self-confidence and initiative. Psychologist Arthur Combs (31), and his colleagues in Supervision of Curriculum Development of the National Education Association state that a child can then dare to try, and can say "let's try" to others. In this way, Combs points out, an occasional mistake or failure will not be a threat to the child but an invitation to think things over and try to do better next time.

This personal foundation should be established before formally launching the child into the world of schooling with its many distractions, its adjustments to a variety of adults and peers, and its pressures to succeed. For children do not learn easily if they are afraid of failure, and this fear is natural if they are not ready. This is certainly obvious to many parents who have tried to start their children on violin or piano lessons at the ages of 5, 6 or even 7. A concert violinist, himself a teacher of the violin, recently confided to us that he is sorry he started his 6-year-olds in a famed violin course for young children. Such tasks, requiring a coordination of the eyes, hands and sometimes the feet, are difficult to learn until the child has reached his integrated maturity level. Attempting such lessons too early often results in frustration and failure as well as loss of interest in further learning.

Learning failure is not the only problem associated with overtaxing of the young brain. A number of public school teachers and administrators are convinced that much delinquency originates in this way. While working as a visiting scientist at the National Institute of Mental Health, Dr. Anneliese Pontius (118), New York University psychiatrist, became convinced of the real possibility of creating anxiety, frustration and delinquent behavior by starting children in school before they are ready. She concluded that we are spending too much time on the basic skills at early ages, when we should be developing sound character qualities. It appears to her that we are more bent on creating moral cripples and ethical retards than on children who have a sound value system. Social and emotional maturity—including spiritual values—provide cornerstones on which maximum intellectual development must be based. Otherwise, the brighter a child is, the more dangerous he will be.

One of the best ways for parents to help in their children's social development is to become involved with them in the daily chores and activities of the home. Such lessons of love and responsibility take time and patience, but in performing duties about the home, children learn how to work and how to relate to work. Even in babyhood, the child can help mother make the bed by fluffing the pillows or straightening the blankets. The parents' patience in sharing these duties will be richly rewarded as the child develops a positive sense of self-worth. And as the child grows older, his involvement with household chores can be wisely expanded. Before he is ready for primary school, he can be a positive asset in carrying out the daily duties of the home. Many children are setting the table and removing the dishes by age 3 or 4, and washing them and putting them away by age 5 or 6. And some children—boys and girls—are trained to prepare an entire meal or wash the car thoroughly by 7 or 8. Some of the best bread we have ever tasted was baked by an 8-year-old. The time parents invest in this kind of education brings the nearest thing to happy and trouble-free futures, *especially if the parents work with the children.* In addition, the child is learning information traditionally associated only with the school experience. He may read from cereal boxes or count cups and spoons when setting the table. He delights in measuring ingredients for recipes. He enjoys weekly trips to the supermarket, where he begins to learn how to price foods.

Students of child behavior have observed that the supermarket provides another valuable experience: The child learns that he has no right to take what he has not purchased—even a little piece of candy—or that if anything is damaged by him, he must pay for it. This is a good opportunity for teaching that for every action, there is a reaction or result that will bring sorrow or happiness.

In a series of experiments, which we reported on at the 1960 White House Conference on Children and Youth (103), we found that, in general, those children who have such daily experiences in the home and related to the home exhibit higher achievement and fewer behavioral problems than those who do not. The child who is involved in home duties feels needed and finds self-respect in carrying his share of the family load. The indulged child has little opportunity for gaining such a self-concept.

Mothers often underestimate the child's ability to entertain himself. They feel that they have to constantly provide amusement. In so doing, they unconsciously induce in the child a desire and demand for more entertainment. This parental concern amounts to indulgence. It is not the product of love, but rather of parental fears of inadequacy. Don't be like the hospital nurses who wake up their patients to give them sleeping pills. The wise mother realizes that interference or indulgence makes her the prisoner of the child, builds resentment in the child and makes him indifferent toward her. Parents, therefore, might well reassess their methods of relating to their children. Involving children in home duties is far more productive than spending time in entertaining them, dressing them up or otherwise indulging them. This is what Benjamin Franklin meant when he said that "An hour's industry will do more to produce cheerfulness, suppress evil humors and retrieve your affairs than a month's moaning."

Little children must, of course, have much time for play. Common sense should be used in assigning chores. Sometimes the parent who requires a child's help in the home is considered cruel, especially when the work interferes with community play. Yet such a parent may actually be providing the greater love.

It is conventional to view love as an act rather than a principle of life. Some parents don't understand that real love is the reason behind an act, rather than the act itself. They operate on a principle of withholding love when a child fails: "Mother can't love you when you do that." Yet this is often the very time children need love the most. Teachers often impose similar restrictions on children. Both parents and teachers, however, frequently produce an effect opposite of what they intended. Children often become less certain, more rigid, less secure, when treated in this manner.

Small youngsters, like many older children and

adults, are in constant need of reassurance. Every child should have frequent success experiences, even of the simplest kinds, and even if the parent or teacher has to deliberately set the stages for them. The duller or less responsible a child appears to be, the greater should be the adult's effort to induce feelings of success in him. Give him something within his ability range that no one else in the family or class is doing. Help him do it well. Then let him show and tell. Such achievements, however small, should receive appreciation. These children are finding their "sea legs," developing balance, and they need that special support. Opportunities are found in every home and every school, and they come in a thousand ways.

If a parent wants a happy child and really loves him, he will wisely and consistently *require* obedience. He values the obedience of love and the sharing of responsibility as the best building blocks for young characters. Firm, reasonable insistence on obedience takes extra effort. But it is one of the greatest and kindest gifts a parent can give.

Some parents, in desperation, send their problems to the preschool, hoping that the teacher may be able to do what they could not do, or are too lazy or undisciplined to do. They want freedom without responsibility, which is more license than liberty—a distortion of freedom and a violation of the child's liberties. In some cases, a wise teacher and the social pressure of the school group do induce improvement in a child's behavior. Yet, if a child returns to a home in which he is the victim of inconsistency and indulgence, he will be even further confused and will eventually be alienated from his parents.

The income level of the family may make a difference in the developmental methods used by the parent, but the child need not be a prisoner of his parent's income. In a ghetto program in Flint, Michigan, Mildred Smith (136) found that about 90 per cent of the families responded to her suggestion to set aside a quiet time at home for reading aloud with their children. When the program was renewed, 99 per cent of the parents voiced their approval that it be continued. In addition, the researchers found that the educator's role should be centered more in helping the young child in the home than in moving him into school—by teaching parents, rather than by assuming responsibilities.

The years from birth to the attainment of a balanced maturity of the child's faculties—his integrated maturity level—are incredibly productive in providing background for the rest of the child's life. Few attitudes and values developed in these early years will later change significantly. It is commonly conceded that, during these years, parents are the most important influence in the lives of young children. But when parents lack knowledge and security, or are too busy or uninterested, we have a potentially deprived child. Some parents may reason that "it won't happen to our child." Let them take time to speak to responsible parents of teenagers, most of whom wish they could do the job over again. Almost to a parent, they will express the wish that they had known more about children and had spent more time with their youngsters during their early years.

Parents can know more about their children, and they can choose to take the time to be with them. This may be considered an old-fashioned, backward way of doing things, especially now that so much public effort is focused on children, rather than on educating parents and parents-to-be for their responsibilities toward those children. Certainly, the public should have concern for children, but we definitely feel that more effort and money should be directed toward helping parents in the home, rather than bringing children to school. Otherwise the potential damage to our concept of family and society may be too great.

As Annikki Suviranta (142), a leading Finnish home economist, astutely observed:

> In the industrialized State, education is being shifted more and more to the community, starting from increasingly younger ages. Nowadays parents have very little say in what their children are taught. Sometimes they don't even know what they're being taught. In other words, education is becoming totalitarian—something imposed from the top downwards.

7.

Time and the Senses

From the time the child is born, parents should be concerned with providing for the balanced development of his brain. This is not as complicated as it sounds. Nor does it call for intellectual stimulation through typical preschool or school-type activities. The small child's learning depends on the harmonious development of many parts of the brain, such as the "centers" of vision, hearing and touch, and the systematic mixing or integration of their functions. Though educational plans and laws are made with specific abilities in mind, in general educational planners and legislators give inadequate attention to the development of the child's entire learning system.

If your child does not develop some abilities as rapidly as others, or if he trails the neighbor's children in certain skills, don't necessarily assume that he is retarded.

If you have serious doubts, see his physician. But normally, there is little reason to worry. Certain functions of his brain may not yet be fully developed for his age. The important need here is patience. Give your child's brain time to develop in all aspects. For example, at a certain stage he may be able to hear better than he can see. Or he may show a greater disposition for touching, feeling or handling things than for hearing you accurately.

Such a lag in maturation of a brain function does not usually imply brain damage or other disability. However, if a child is required to develop basic skills in reading, writing, arithmetic and language arts before the various functions of the brain balance out, he often will give the impression that he is retarded or mentally disabled. Such "learning disabilities" frequently disappear with thoughtful parenting, when the child is withdrawn from kindergarten or primary school and given freedom from studies for another year or two. But if he is kept at these learning tasks before he is ready for them, he may develop any one of many problems associated with learning failure. Some of these problems are as simple as hesitation, confusion of words or reversal of letters; some may be more complex nervous disorders, such as stuttering, stammering or severe psychological disturbances.

We must realize that the child who is required to learn things before he is ready may quickly tire of them. Or he may become anxiety-ridden and so frustrated that he will not try at all. In his frustration, he will turn often to other activities, which may be destructive. Logical questions then arise. When do these neurophysiological abilities usually balance out in the child's development? When can the child's ability to see, hear and touch be effectively coordinated? Some scientists (12) suggest that these abilities develop most rapidly between the ages of 5 and 7 and reach a point of efficient functioning around age 10 or 11. At this age, the various aspects of a child's development have reached a level of maturity and integration that make learning relatively easy.

For more than 25 years, physiologists have been studying the brain intensively through electroencephalography. In the early years many of their results were questioned. But with the improvement of equipment and technique, the study of brain waves suggests many answers to long-standing questions about brain development.

For the first year and a half or so of life, the young child's brain tends to demonstrate slow "delta" rhythms. After the first year and until the child is through adolescence, the character of these "brain waves" changes progressively. Brain specialists believe that these waves come primarily from the superficial layers of the cortex, interacting with deeper brain regions and with itself. They suggest that this integration or balance among these brain regions is not complete for some time. While the myelination—sheathing of the nerve fibers of the brain— may continue for 30 or more years, the balance between the two sides, or hemispheres, of the brain probably is achieved much earlier. Dr. David Metcalf (99) of the University of Colorado Medical School believes the division of labor between the two sides is probably established somewhere *between 7 and 9* years of age.

We should not be surprised if the young child is more an "emotional creature" than a reasoning one. There may be more emotion than reason involved in his decisions and actions. Normally, as he grows older, he should be able to reason more and better. But he will not be able to do so consistently—as shown in the next chapter—until he is 8 to 10 or older. He may, for instance, be told precisely why he should go to bed early, but this explanation simply may not make sense to him. His reason is dominated by his emotions. And, as most of us have observed, the person of any age who is dominated by his emotions is usually regarded as immature in that respect. As a child becomes more and more a reasoning person he can more consistently explain the "why" of things. This ability is basic for learning to read, to do arithmetic, to spell.

Occasionally, questions have been raised as to whether stimulations make the brain mature faster or letting the brain mature first makes school easier. The former would affirm the need for early schooling; the latter would deny it. So far, this question has not been fully answered. Both views may be true in some respects. Yet, in terms of related research, early stimulation appears to involve greater risk to the young child than allowing him more time to mature.

Studies have demonstrated a variety of significant changes in brain maturation between ages 7 and 11. Some of these changes are in the brain's structure, others are in its chemistry and still others in its electrical potential. A number of neurophysiologists and psychiatrists (32, 88, 108, 155, 156, 157, 106, 99, 100) believe that the actual structural development of the brain and its function in learning are very closely related. Findings by Dr. Paul Yakovlev (156) of Harvard relating to structure and function of the brain, and clinical studies by child psychiatrist Humberto Nagera (106) of the University of Michigan agree closely with the conclusions of Swiss psychologist Jean Piaget (116) that the young child's brain should not be hurried in the learning process. Rather, it should be given time and the best possible climate in which to develop. With this complex process of brain maturation comes an increasing ability to handle problems and to perform learning skills in a sound way.

But what kind of climate brings the best balance in maturation? It is difficult to demonstrate that the child's brain develops better in one place than another. However, some interesting animal experiments have been made that give some indication of what may be the best environment. A Berkeley team of University of California scientists, headed by Mark Rosenzweig (124), experimented with rats to determine under what circumstances these animals developed the best myelination.

The first group of rats was placed under standard laboratory conditions in clean cages with plenty of food and water. The second group was housed in an enriched environment—in cages where they had not only plenty of food, but a variety of things to play with and which might provide more security. The playthings were changed daily so the rats would not be bored. The third group was separated so that each rat lived alone in a cage. Still another group of rats was set in a natural environment, where they could play among rocks, grass and twigs, and dig in the dirt. In this last group, it was found that the rats, who had not been in such an environment for many generations, very quickly dug holes and behaved as rats are normally expected to do in a natural environment.

The brain of each rat was studied for development and structure. The examination showed that the rats in the enriched laboratory environment had much thicker and better sheathing of their brain fibers than those in the sterile cages or those who were by themselves. But the rats who were left to run in the natural habitat were altogether better in their myelination. It can be inferred from this experiment that the more natural and free the animal's environment, the better the quality the brain development is likely to be. It is not practical to make similar studies of the human brain, but the Rosenzweig data fits remarkably into the known research from other areas of child development. A good home with reasonable freedom and solitude does seem to produce the better-developed child.

VISION

One fact well accepted by neurophysiologists and most eye specialists is that the eye is an integral part of the brain. Doctors James C. Chalfant and Margaret A. Scheffelin (27) describe the retina of the eye as "an outward extension of the cerebral cortex."

Teachers have commonly noted that children of 6 or younger are often not able to see well enough to read properly. Frequently, this is also noted in 7-year-olds. Yet there are those who argue that children should be encouraged to read at the age of 2 or 3. Some researchers and scholars insist that there is strong evidence that a child's eyes are not physiologically ready for continual and consistent reading until he is at least 8 or even older. They also point to another question in this controversy: What is actually involved in the process of reading? Some educators believe that reading involves a response primarily from the eyes. In other words, reading appears to be a simple visual process. Others point out, however, that reading is a much more complex process. It involves many parts of the brain and requires that these parts work together instantly and implicitly. They call this the *visual perception process* or the *visual learning factor*.

This visual perception process is highly complex. In order to understand what he reads, a child must be able to connect new thoughts with things he has already learned. Then he must retrieve what he learned earlier from his memory and integrate it with the new information. So he is constantly analyzing and synthesizing, or putting things together. He must also do this in learning arithmetic, spelling and other subjects if he is to do an effective job. And the more abstract the material is, the more complex is the learning task. Some school children are unable to distinguish letters within words or parts of letters. For example, to some children an "F" is not distinguishable from an "E"; or they do not see much difference between a "p" and a "b" or a "d." For a child to read well, he must be able to visualize the shapes of both letters and words. But to do this, he must be able to reason out their structure and retain them in his mind, so that he can build other words on them in the future. Not until he can reason in this way can he read without strain. And this reasoning process does not begin to be consistent (as we will note more fully in the next chapter) until about age 8 or later.

As long ago as the turn of the century, famed American philosopher John Dewey (35) quoted eye specialists in noting that children's eyes are made primarily for distant vision or for looking at large objects. To require the child to concentrate on near work or upon small objects for any length of time, he reasoned, would create undue nervous strain. He estimated that children should not be required to make these refined and cramped adjustments until about age 8. Otherwise, he noted, there would be a sad record of injured nervous systems and of muscular disorders and distortions.

Throughout the years, many of the nation's leading child specialists have concurred with these findings. In the thirties, Columbia University's Luella Cole (29) stated that 8 was soon enough for a child to begin to read printed symbols on any regular basis. In the forties, Doctors Arnold Gesell and Frances Ilg (50) suggested caution in placing demands on young eyes for reading and arithmetic. They indicated that unreasonable exactions may be the source of poor attitudes toward study of these subjects. Eminent reading specialist Lillian Gray (55) pointed out in the fifties and sixties that some children are not able to fixate on objects at close range, as required by reading and arithmetic, until they are at least 7 or 8 years old. And seven decades after John Dewey's observation, psychologist Louise Ames (4) noted that visual or perceptual problems were one of the common causes of school failure.

Many educators consider the child's mental age the key to his maturity. It appears, however, that it is not necessarily the crucial factor in reading. A child may actually be very bright and may even appear to read words well, yet not be perceptive in his reading or able to read without damage to his eyes and his nervous system. His brain development may not be sufficient for him to reason out the relationships required in reading. His eyes may be physically unable to determine the forms and shapes of words without strain. According to some ophthalmologists, a child who is forced to read under these circumstances may have an accommodation spasm. Such an adjustment spasm can set up conditions that will lead to near-sightedness at a time when the child should still be far-sighted.

The tissues of young children's eyes, up to about age 8 or 9, are softer or more plastic than older eyes. For example, the sclera, or outer covering of the eyeball, can be drawn out of normal shape by undue strain (71). Until the young child's eyes have moved beyond this stage of plasticity, he should not read much, but should wait until his visual system is stabilized. And considering the possibility of damage to his eyes and his nervous system, not to mention his motivation, the brighter the child is, the greater may be the risk of a regular reading program before age 8.

In a study of students in grades one through six, optometrist H. M. Coleman (30) found that approximately half of all the pupils he tested had visual, perceptual or refractive problems severe enough to cause difficulties in reading. Significantly, 70% of these disabled readers were boys; it is commonly understood that boys trail girls 6 to 12 months in developmental maturity. Thus, Stanley Krippner (87), an authority on problems of vision and reading, found in his studies that nearly 90% of his disabled readers were boys.

An Austin, Texas, ophthalmologist, Henry Hilgartner (71), approached the problem from another point of view, studying the effect of close work on visual development. He and his father, also an eye specialist, kept careful clinical records over a period of more than 50 years for all 8- to 12-year-old children that they examined. Hilgartner noted that in the early 1900's, nearly eight children were far-sighted to every one who was near-sighted. This is consistent with well-established findings of eye specialists that for children between the ages of 8 and 12, far-sightedness or hyperopia, is normal.

In 1907–1908, the Texas legislature reduced the school entrance age from 8 to 7. By 1930, there were only two children with normal vision to each child with abnormal vision. In 1930–1931, the legal school age in Texas was dropped to 6. Hilgartner found that by 1940 the ratio of normal to abnormal children was one to one instead of the earlier seven or eight to one. With the advent of television—which encouraged even more close vision— the problem became more serious, and by 1962 the ratio was one normal or far-sighted child to five abnormal. Hilgartner presented his report in 1963. When he wrote us in 1972, he noted that he was seeing very few hyperopic young people under 21 years of age. Frank Newton (110), a Dallas ophthalmologist who made a similar study, said that his findings agreed largely with Hilgartner's. And Newton says myopia is still on the increase.

Critics will argue, however, that there is not that much reading or close work for a 6-year-old in kindergarten or first grade. For these, Hilgartner has an answer (71):

The educators, at least the ones I have talked to, say that in the first grade of school, there is little book work or reading that the child experiences. They say that the child plays and he is taught to draw and he begins to learn about the birds and bees. For the sake of peace, I will concede that the actual amount of reading the first grade or kindergarten child does is nil. However, I will not concede that he does not use his eyes excessively for near work, while in the school room. I make the charge that most of the morning he is looking at pictures, making drawings, or watching the teacher draw pictures on the nearby blackboard.

During the 3 or 4 hours that the beginner, age 6, is in school he is using all the ocular muscles for accommodation and convergence, in order to see the pictures, drawings, etc. If he were outdoors, playing . . . he would not be using his eyes excessively for close work. The internal and external recti, the superior and inferior recti, as well as the obliques would not be working excessively to make the child see a single object.

Because the visual mechanism of a 6-year-old is unstable, children have a difficult time moving their eyes back and forth on a page. Primary teachers commonly observe that a child who reads at 5 or 6 will often follow words with his finger and will frequently skip a line, while an older child usually has much less trouble. Cole (29) observed that some children who cannot adjust to the difficulties of near vision find reading so uncomfortable that they give up trying to learn.

There is even more extensive evidence that abnormal near-sightedness is caused through early reading and other near work. Dr. Tikasi Sato (128) of Japan has found that myopia results from the effort of the young child to adapt to near work; and Dr. George Milkie (101), Director of Professional Development of the American Optometric Association, states that near work as a cause of myopia is one on which all clinicians agree. Their findings are also supported, in essence, by Dr. Francis Young (159), Washington State University psychologist, who observed how the eye adapts to its environmental conditions and showed that environmental factors play a greater role in the development of myopia than do hereditary factors.

Dr. Young found that monkeys kept in limited environments without the possibility of distant vision developed near-sightedness while those allowed freedom of distant vision generally did not. He also found that Alaskan Eskimo children who in recent years have been placed in school have a significantly higher likelihood of developing myopia than their parents and grandparents who did not go to school. These findings suggest that it is not wise to stress close vision until the visual system nears full development, and that for its best development, the system needs the active use of distant vision. Later schooling does not eliminate the possibility of such eye strain but greatly reduces its likelihood.

HEARING

A number of scientists have discovered that hearing, like vision, may not be mature enough for the child to read well until he is 8 or 9 years old. While examining his daughters for possible reading problems, Dr. Jerome Rosner (125), an optometrist at the University of Pittsburgh, began to realize that hearing may also be important in learning to read. After finding that a number of his young patients with reading problems had adequate vision and did not need glasses, and then after making a careful audial study of these children, using standardized tests, he suggested that vision is not the only crucial factor, but that learning to read also depends heavily upon auditory skills. Apart from the use of the eyes to see words, in order for a child to read well, for example, he must be able to distinguish between such similar sounds as "k" (kuh) and "g" (guh) or "p" (puh) and "b" (buh). Further, he must be able to hear the entire word and perceive its meaning within the sentence, or he is unlikely to remember it. Yet University of Chicago's Joseph Wepman (151) says that some children cannot readily distinguish and remember sounds until the end of the eighth year. Another University of Chicago researcher, Anne Morency (105), agrees, noting that the growing child develops a steady increase in ability to discriminate between sounds.

Until recent years, the importance of hearing to the reading process had been less widely appreciated than that of vision. Yet nearly all adults will recall, often with a chuckle, their misuse of sounds as children. Recently, at a Christmas party, a group of mothers told us stories about their 5- and 6-year olds who were not yet able without help to hear and understand the meaning of the first sentence of the Lord's Prayer: "Our Father which art in heaven, hallowed be Thy name." Howard, a delightful 5-year-old, heard, "Howard, be thy name." To another it was, "How did you know my name?" And to a New York child, the petition to "Lead us not into temptation" came out as "Lead us not into Penn Station." Even adults sometimes have hearing discrimination problems that carry over from childhood, so that "picture" becomes "pitcher" or "nuclear" becomes "new-kewler."

INTERSENSORY PERCEPTION

For a child to develop maturity in any one of the senses alone is not adequate for ease of learning. It is important that all his senses be reasonably well developed, for pleasant learning requires the integration and cooperation of not only vision and hearing, but also of touch, smell and taste. Almost from birth, for example, children learn a great deal through the sense of touch; but according to the late Dr. Harold Birch and his colleague, Dr. Arthur

Lefford (12), it is not until they have reached the maturity level of about 8 years or so that they usually are able to integrate visual learning and hearing with the sense of touch.

This complex integration of the senses requires the simultaneous function of almost countless brain connections. Since the reasonably mature cooperation of the senses does not normally emerge until at least 8 years of age, children who are forced earlier into tasks where these senses must work evenly or in balance may appear brain-damaged or handicapped when actually they are not. A. Jean Ayres (6) a professor of education at the University of Southern California suggests, on the basis of both research and clinical experience, that many learning disorders derive from the lack of integration of the senses and the balanced development of the brain. Marianne Frostig (46), director of the Marianne Frostig Center of Educational Therapy at Los Angeles, agrees. We suggest the possibility that by simply waiting for the child to develop reasonable levels of maturity, as suggested earlier, many children may avoid serious learning problems altogether.

Vision researcher Homer Hendrickson (68) underscores the importance of readiness for learning, noting that eye difficulties result not so much from faulty eyes themselves as from how eyes work with each other, with the brain and in coordination with all the child's senses. A good example of the advantages of intersensory cooperation is seen in a child who is learning to play a musical instrument. One study (149) found that the average child is mentally ready for violin lessons at the age of 8.3 years and is physically mature enough at 8.2. Yet teachers agreed that not until an average age of 9.5 years does the child become truly responsive to music study. And these teachers found that the best progress of all is made at 11.5

years, by which age the child is able to coordinate mind, ear and body.

No one knows exactly when or how the very young child learns, or exactly how much he knows. The shift from the shock of a slap on the bottom at birth to the pleasure of the first suck at the breast may bring his first experience in confusion. Obviously, there is enough incidental and unavoidable confusion throughout his learning experience without subjecting him to unnecessary anxiety and frustration by forcing him to learn before he is ready. A well-developed brain is of primary importance for learning, for learning is based upon the condition and use of the senses that are based there.

8.

Learning to Reason

Parents and scholars long have been aware of the rapid development of the young child's mind. Frances Xavier, the sixteenth-century Jesuit leader and missionary, declared, "Give me the children until they are seven and anyone may have them afterwards." Today's learning psychologists use the word cognition (or cognitive) to refer to the mental aspect of child development. Cognition, defined as "the act or process of knowing including both awareness and judgment" by *Webster's Dictionary,* refers to the ability of an individual to perceive and to develop learning skills. Often, in the language of the psychologist, *cognitive* is contrasted with *affective,* which refers mainly to the child's socio-emotional condition or development.

Recently, as a result of the research and conclusions of such psychologists as Benjamin Bloom (14) and Jerome

Bruner (21), many educators and parents have become excited about the possibilities of being able to teach their children almost anything during their first 4 or 5 years. This, in turn, has led to the widespread fear that if the children are not stimulated cognitively during these years they might not reach their maximum potential. Children certainly do learn fast in their early years, and they can be taught many things. Some children, for instance, learn the ABC's as early as 18 months or 2 years. Yet they may learn these letters and words without understanding what they are learning. A few years later, however, when learning skills can be acquired with much greater ease and speed, they will know the meaning behind these symbols.

Experiments have shown that children can be taught to climb stairs almost as soon as they can walk; but at such an early age they may also develop fears that later will be handicaps. Or, with a good deal of patient, consistent teaching, 2- or 3-year-olds can learn to swing; but panic and frustration often accompany their eventual success. Yet if one waits a few months until the child is ready for these experiences, he will have developed the necessary coordination to learn these tasks without any instruction and with little or no pressure. And he is far less likely to develop anxieties and frustrations in the process. Premature teaching often results not only in damage to the child, but also in an enormous amount of wasted effort by parents and teachers who feel compelled to teach skills or facts too early.

Much is being done these days to try to compensate young children for the losses they may have suffered because of a deprived background or because of other handicaps. While some of these efforts have helped the children socially, emotionally or culturally, few, if any, have had any enduring effect as measured by later scholastic performance. In a widely published research analysis, Arthur Jensen (78) concludes that compensatory education —to help the child recoup his losses or compensate for his handicaps—"has been tried and it apparently has failed." On the other hand, Harvard's Jerome Kagan (81) believes compensatory programs have been neither adequately developed nor adequately appraised. One is forced to draw the conclusion that thus far these programs have not clearly proven to compensate educationally for the child's disadvantaged years in a deprived environment. Compensatory education deserves much more study. It may be that a focus on homing instead of schooling is the answer. By mid-1974 over 200 Head Start programs had already incorporated the principles of Home Start into their activities.

Some believe that parents and educators should be less concerned about making up early losses. On the basis of research, experimentation and application of growth principles, psychologist William Rohwer (123) suggests that for many children efforts to increase independent perception or cognitive ability are more likely to succeed ". . . if they are delayed . . . until near the end of the elementary school years." Rohwer (122) also suggests that all of the learning ". . . necessary for success in meeting high school demands can be accomplished in only two or three years—the junior high school years." If prescribed instruction were delayed until those years, he believes, many children might achieve greater academic success. Sixty 6- and 9-year-old black children from Prince Edward County, Virginia, a community which had been without public schools for 4 years, were compared with sixty 6- and 9-year-old black children of similar socio-economic level who had received regular schooling. As expected there was no difference in performance between the two groups of 6-year-olds. But researchers were surprised to find that the 9-year-olds who had never been to school performed as well as those who had three years of schooling.

Psychiatrist J. T. Fisher (44) supports Rohwer from both personal and clinical experience. Dr. Fisher started school at 13, finished high school at 16. He was "disillusioned in later years to discover that this was no particular proof of genius." Rather, he had to agree with psychologists who "have demonstrated that a normal child commencing his academic education in adolescence can soon reach the same point of progress he would have achieved by starting to school at 5 or 6 years of age." (1951:14) And a recent Stanford Research Institute study by Meredith L. Robinson (121) points to the likelihood that the early adolescent years, from 10 to 14, may be the time when most children finally develop the full range of their capacities, or in effect, reach their integrated maturity level.

In other words, parents need not fear that they are wasting their children's early years if they do not send them to school. On the contrary, the children left to invent or work things out for themselves in a relatively free environment will probably become more creative persons and better at solving problems. Piaget (115) says that ". . . the problem of learning is not at all to be confused with that of spontaneous development even though spontaneous development always comprises learning."

Piaget has often been asked whether or not he endorses American programs that provide earlier and earlier schooling. According to John L. Phillip (114), when Piaget was asked whether the child's brain can be speeded up, he called this the "American question." Piaget thought ". . . it probably can but probably should not be speeded up." He does not think the best time is the least time, but would rather see children develop fully and naturally than be hurried.

One day while we were living in Japan, our 5-year-old

daughter came skipping into the house with an unusually beautiful red rosebud. "Look, Mommy," she spoke happily, "I'm blooming it." Indeed she was. Her little fingers were delicately pulling back each petal one by one in a remarkably orderly way. We waited until she had finished "blooming" her rosebud. Then we brought to the table another rose which had bloomed naturally. Even a 5-year-old could quickly see that her rose had been fractured and bruised, however tender her blooming. The other rose was serene and unspoiled from opening in nature's own way.

The "wisdom" of forcing a child's intellect has little basis either in research or in common sense. Usually, stimulating anything to go faster simply because it can go fast will merely insure an earlier breakdown. This is implicitly true whenever we try to rush nature, and it is especially true in the development of children. Children should be permitted to "unfold" as naturally as a flower.

Thoughtful mothers and fathers often wonder when children should start making their own decisions and begin to think for themselves. There is no single starting and stopping place. Rather, the process is a gradual one that begins during the child's first two or three years and may vary widely from child to child. Within the limits of his ability to reason and to be responsible for consequences, the child should be permitted to practice decision-making early. Yet parents should not let their child be rushed.

Piaget and Hans Furth suggest that children arrive fully at the age of reason later rather than earlier. Reports on Piaget's (67) experiments indicate that some youngsters did not become consistent reasoners until they were nearly 11 years old. Hans Furth, a psychology professor from the Catholic University of America, tells of typical reasoning problems in 8-year-olds: One 8-year-old boy concluded that since the mayor of Washington, D.C., was

Mr. Washington, Philadelphia's mayor must be Mr. Philadelphia. Another 8-year-old assumed that Switzerland's Lake Geneva must have been created by the founders of Geneva "because builders always come before things are built." According to Piaget (116), decisions involving a combination of *several ideas* ". . . are not easily made until eleven or twelve years of age."

If parents become aware of how reason develops gradually in their child, they can develop the ability to reason with him. But until the child arrives fully at the age of reason, the parent must consistently share the decision-making. This sharing should not be passed on lightly to others who do not know the child and his background well, and who cannot deal with him consistently on a one-to-one basis. If the sharing is kept on a simple basis and is done in a warm, responsive and systematic way throughout the early years, the child will be in a much better position, socially and emotionally as well as cognitively, to make decisions in his later years.

Even though a young child may be eager, bright and interested in everything around him, he is still immature and cannot be expected to learn or behave in the manner of an older person. David Elkind (40) describes some of the mental limitations of the young child: (1) He is naturally egocentric because of an inability to put himself in another's place or take another's point of view. (2) Many times there is a discrepancy between what he thinks and what he says. He may use many words and phrases that he does not really understand, and he may somehow give the impression that he knows more than he actually does. (3) The preschooler has a difficult time following rules that adults impose upon him—rules that a few years later he can understand with ease. When children are corrected for things that they thought they were doing right, they become confused. Therefore, a parent should be sure that a child knows why he is being scolded or punished. And while there should be firmness and consistency, children should not be spanked in anger. Likewise, when children cannot reach the learning expectations of adults, parents should take pains not to become discouraged and give up helping their child.

Often parents and teachers make judgments that do not take into account a child's background. Jerome Kagan (80) says, "There are few dumb children in the world if one classifies them from the perspective of the community of adaptation, but millions of dumb children if one classifies them from the perspective of another society." As an example, it may have been very important to an early American Indian to know how to track animals or to make tepees; it was not important for him to know logarithms, much less the prose of Shakespeare or the diagraming of a sentence. By the standards of our industrialized society he knew nothing, but by the standards of his own people, he may have been highly adaptive and, indeed, very bright. Conversely, children of industrial society may not appear bright by Indian standards.

Some parents and teachers confuse *learning skills* with *development.* A child should first be free to develop naturally. Then learning skills can be acquired more easily when he is ready. A child tends to absorb knowledge by exploring his world and actively experimenting with real things. He learns much more in this way than in being taught passively. And he is less likely to fail. The so-called basic skills of reading, writing and arithmetic must be considered to be strictly secondary to sound basic development of mind, emotions and body.

In a sense, preschool is sometimes an invasion of the child's integrity—it asks him to make adjustments that he cannot readily make, and forces him to play a game of dishonesty, to pretend when he is actually unable to do a good school job. With reasonable direction and with reasonable freedom, a normal child can learn in *his* way what should be learned at each stage of his development. When he thus learns without pressure, he becomes eager for new experiences. He can absorb new learning much faster than when constantly trying to conform to others' expectations.

If the young child is provided the best possible environment, his appetite for learning will give him all the motivation and food for thought that he needs. Yale's Edward Zigler (161) points out, "You do not need to force learning upon a child; learning is an inherent feature of being a human being." The development of intelligence proceeds spontaneously although it can be slowed or advanced by the environment.

The very small child has little concept of space or distances. He seldom is aware of the passing of time. Schedules are out of the question for his private operations. He understands little about how things relate to each other. Then, gradually, he begins to put things together. He finds that water and dirt make mud, and that you cannot build tunnels in sand that is dry. During his first five or six years, he is very busy learning basic ideas or concepts concerning colors and textures, tastes and smells and length and height. Sometime around age 8 or later, he begins to put his thoughts together in a logical way. He discovers that because a glass is tall and narrow, it does not necessarily hold more water than one that is short and wide. As Furth (47) has noted, "These general concepts of the developing intelligence evolve whether the child goes to school or not."

The ability to reason from cause to effect appears to grow sharply between the ages of 7 and 11, the years that Piaget (116) calls operational. Gradually the growing child becomes able to think problems through in his head; and it is somewhere during this period that he begins to read with understanding.

The process of reading also involves many other aspects of the child's personality. Success can depend upon whether he feels the need to read, or upon the quality of the printed word as well as upon his readiness to understand those thoughts he finds in print. He may read words without much understanding, or he may read and think through thoughts in an effective way, reasoning as he moves along. Reading with understanding should always be the goal of parents and teachers.

If we are to be satisfied simply with word reading, then the 2-year-old can learn to "read," seeing words as he would pictures. Soon he can read "STOP" at intersections—but without understanding what STOP means. Furthermore, in the primary grades, these early readers may not have the necessary experience to decode and process information in an allotted time. Because they then cannot read or do their arithmetic fast enough and well enough, they often become frustrated and get an "I'm dumb" complex, when actually, they are bright but not ready. They then will often either become troublemakers or sit silently or become dyslexic or become categorized as retarded. In other words, they seemingly and subconsciously set out to become exactly what they were diagnosed to be—retarded. And we diagnose others as hyperkinetic or wild, when we have simply built the frustrations into them.

To take a child through the experience of reading when he cannot exercise reasoning is an exercise in futility. Reading specialists often find that children who have been forced in this way to read at early ages become frustrated and lose their motivation. Frequently, they level out on a motivational plateau at about grade three or four. They lose interest. The great excitement for school is gone. And they may never regain their interest unless they are fortunate enough to have the help of a reading specialist well versed in child psychology and motivation.

There is little wonder that the federal government's Right to Read program claims that there are 7,000,000 youngsters with reading problems. This program of the Department of Health, Education and Welfare has effectively publicized the need for providing reading programs for all, regardless of handicap, and has promoted remedial and developmental reading programs at local, state and national levels. Those organizations and individuals concerned with this right should be among the foremost to insure that schooling is not rushed. Children who experience frustration commonly turn away from school to seek satisfaction elsewhere. Here are the seeds of delinquency.

Reading specialist Nila Banton Smith (137) believes that those who advocate regular reading programs for young children do not understand the nature of the process of reading. She says, "For one thing, they seem to consider reading as a growth in itself apart from all other growths, as a separate strand of learning that can be pulled out and worked on whenever the adult decides to teach a child to read. . . . Some people seem to think that when a child can pronounce a word appearing in print he is reading."

Malcolm Douglass (36) stresses the importance of recognizing that reading is primarily a thinking process. He says that we could probably reduce our reading problems to about 2% if we would delay formal reading instruction to the age of 9 or 10. This view is consistent with the experience of Scandinavian schools, where children have historically entered no earlier than age 7 and where reading problems are relatively rare.

It is difficult not to conclude that the young child needs the early years for a normal blossoming period before he is ready for any serious approach to the skills of reading, writing and arithmetic. There is little evidence to support the effectiveness of even the normal skills readiness programs in preschools. The young child who is allowed the freedom to mature in his home environment will typically be a better balanced, more stable, more sociable and higher achieving child and, very likely, a better adjusted person than the child who must leave the home for other care.

9.

Comparing Early and Late Starters

Schools do not serve children or society effectively when they expect children to learn the basic skills before they are ready. Children who are successful and happy in a school situation experience satisfaction from, and are challenged by, learning. This excitement about learning is a natural result of being ready to learn. As Arnold Gesell and Frances Ilg (50) of the Gesell Institute have suggested:

> When the school child was a baby the adult attitudes tended to be more reasonable. One did not say he should walk at this or that age. Feeling confident that he would walk at the most seasonable time, one was more interested to observe the stage and degree of his preliminary development. If reading readiness and walking readiness are ap-

praised on similar grounds, more justice is done to the child.

Children develop at different rates in various facets of their growth. University of Michigan psychologist Willard Olson (113) noted that ". . . children of the same age and the same grade location are regularly found to differ by as much as four or five years in their maturation and their readiness to perform tasks." Twenty-five years later, Harvard's Jerome Kagan (80) expressed the same idea: "Separate maturational factors seem to set the time of emergence of basic functions. Experience can slow down or speed up that emergence by several months or three to four years, but nature will win in the end."

The child's natural rate of development must be recognized by parents and teachers, and by legislators. If attempts are made to force it, the child may suffer permanent damage in the process. But if the child is permitted to develop in a natural way, surrounded by a sound sense of family values, his capacities will, in Kagan's words, "eventually appear in sturdy form."

We are sometimes asked why, when our studies are concerned mostly with preschool ages, we also take time to compare the performance of early and late starters in primary school. There are several reasons:

First, research suggests that developmentally, early childhood encompasses at least the first 8 years, even though by age 8 many children are in the third grade.

Second, if the later starters do better, then we should be cautious about earlier schooling.

Third, if early exposure to the basic skills frequently brings a later indifference to them, we will know to plan programs free from such teaching in those preschools and kindergartens that we must operate.

And fourth, comparing ages for school-entrance-age

studies provides one of the few long-term studies that follow the child's progress through the years, examining his disposition—anxieties, frustrations, motivation—and his achievement.

In nearly every case, these long-term studies favor the later entrant. In fact, we know of no such studies that clearly support the idea of early entrance to school, or that demonstrate that early entrants make significant continuing gains in attitudes, motivation, achievement and social and emotional growth.

There is, however, a substantial body of research that points to strong gains in these very areas by students who are enrolled later. James T. Fisher (44), known in the 1940's and 1950's as the dean of American psychiatrists, at 87 wrote his autobiography, *A Few Buttons Missing*. In it he describes how his father kept him out of school until he was 13. The family had moved from Chicago to Boston, but Jim's father sent him back to Illinois at age 8 to work on a friend's cattle ranch. Dr. Fisher later described the experience.

> It was my father's belief that a healthy mind is a natural by-product of a healthy body; that the world's most potent medicines are to be found in sunshine and clean fresh air and in the waters of a babbling brook, without any aid from an apothecary shop; and that the most important lessons in the world are learned without any aid from books.
>
> "There'll be plenty of time for school and for books later on," he told my mother. "First he must build a strong body and a fine physique. Let him learn to hear the song of the wind and the rustle of leaves and all the music of the prairie, before you send him off to listen to some perspiring fiddle player in a stuffy hall."

Young Fisher returned east to start his schooling at age 13. By the time he was 16, he had completely overtaken the boys of his age, having mastered in three years all the formal education they had acquired in eleven.

We have suggested strongly that children who start later should not be required to go lock-step through the grades, but should be placed with their peers who had started earlier or, at least, should be quickly accelerated to catch up with them. Contrary to a common fear of parents and teachers that late starters will be ridiculed by other students, the late entrants often enjoy distinction and admiration. Says Albert Clark (28) of Battle Creek, Michigan, who started school at age 8, "When I read with the class I did not have to put my fingers on the words like other kids. They thought I was special." As noted earlier, out of about 400 reactions we have received from individuals who started school at 8 or later, only four reported serious problems; and each of these four had been forced to start in the first grade. These 400 late starters also present a surprising unanimity of success and leadership in their professions. While this is hardly a scientific sampling, it is an impressive witness to the importance of readiness for learning and of maturity for motivation.

Many specific experiments have been carried out over the last 50 years that illustrate the difference between the performance of children who go to school earlier and those who remain at home longer.

Inez King (85) studied two groups of children in Oak Ridge, Tennessee, comparing 54 youngsters who were from 5 years, 8 months to 5 years, 11 months old when they started school, with 50 children who started about six months later.

Even though there was only a six- to nine-month difference in ages of these very young children, King found that of the 11 children who repeated a grade, only one had started school after 6 years of age. On the other hand, 19 boys and 16 girls of the younger group appeared to be maladjusted in some way, while only 3 boys and 3 girls from the older group were considered maladjusted. King discovered a noticeable tendency in the younger group toward speech defects, nervous indications and personal and social maladjustments.

Margaret Gott (53) compared 171 California kindergarten children who were about 4 years, 9 months old at enrollment with 171 who entered nearly a year later. She ranked them on a ten-point scale, measuring socio-emotional development. There were four times as many younger children as older in the lowest rank, and nearly twice as many of the younger group in the three lowest ranks combined. Conversely, there were more than twice as many of the older group in the three highest ranks.

We read a clear lesson here for those parents who believe that sending their children to school early tends to socialize them. The opposite appears to be suggested in virtually every comparison of early and late starters. In fact, the child who remains at home with a mother and shares the tasks of the home appears to develop self-respect and a sense of responsibility and values not shared by the child who started school earlier. These values, in turn, seem to bring with them a certain social and emotional stability that is difficult otherwise to achieve. Dr. Gott noted that, according to records and faculty reports, older entrants were judged higher on leadership than younger entrants. For those who are concerned about sending their children to school at an early age because they are very bright, Dr. Gott concluded that two-thirds of the significant differences among children in the higher IQ ranges were in favor of the older children.

In a similar study, H. M. Davis (34), a New Jersey school principal, found that children starting school just six to nine months later received only about two-fifths as many low marks as those who started earlier. He was moved to tell parents, "If your child was born just one day too late and is just unlucky enough to miss entering school this year, the chances are that he is just lucky enough to miss an unhappy school experience and gain a happy one."

During the 1950's and 1960's, Paul Mawhinney (93), Director of Pupil Personnel and other psychologists in Michigan's elite Grosse Pointe School District decided on an experiment to introduce 4- and 5-year-olds into school. For 14 summers a special testing program to select early entrants for kindergarten was carried out. Parents literally fought to have their children accepted and were deeply disappointed and highly critical if they were rejected from this program. Yet at the end of a 14-year period, Mawhinney and his staff found the following to be true:

(1) Nearly one-third of the early entrants turned out to be poorly adjusted.

(2) Only about one out of 20 was judged to be an outstanding leader at the end of the experiment.

(3) Nearly three out of four were considered entirely lacking in leadership.

After only five or six years of this experiment, the chairman of the Grosse Pointe psychologists had grave misgivings. Yet the study continued for nearly nine more years because of pressures from the parents, who insisted on the superiority of their young children. Ultimately, the staff concluded not only that the experiment was a failure in terms of the desirability of sending children to school early, but also that for many of these children it was a very real personal experience in failure, a destruction of their self-image. The children felt that they were not capable of doing what was expected of them, although in fact if they had been allowed to develop normally, their prospects were outstanding. Even worse for many, they appeared to sense that they had not lived up to their parents' expectations, but had disappointed them in a significant way.

In Montclair, New Jersey, John Forester (45), who had been the public school administrator for twenty years, studied 500 school children from kindergarten through high school. He found that those pupils who were very bright but very young at the time of school entrance did not realize their potential. They tended to be physically immature or emotionally unstable, or they would cry easily. And socially, they seldom showed leadership. From junior high school on, 50% of them earned only "C" grades. On the other hand, generally the very bright late-school-entrance group excelled throughout their school careers. Forester noted that ". . . many parents believe that a very bright child will do well in school regardless of his chronological age even if he is younger than the other children in his class. Even some professional educators believe this is true." However, he concluded from his study that ". . . in many cases early entry may result in maladjustment in school, and may even have an adverse effect on adult life."

Throughout these and many other experiments, it was found that the early entrants often had to repeat grades, a pattern that normally would not be expected among brighter youngsters. In the Mawhinney (93) study, approximately one in four of the very bright early school entrants was either below average in school or had to repeat a grade.

Joseph W. Halliwell (63), one of the more prominent of the researchers on the subject of entrance age and school success, found older fourth-grade pupils to be significantly superior to younger fourth graders in reading and in the reading-related areas of spelling and language. If students who had not been promoted had been included in his study, the superiority of the older pupils would have been even more pronounced.

Halliwell (62) later made a relatively comprehensive review of early entrance studies. He concluded that ". . . early entrance to first grade does result in lower achievement throughout the grades when comparisons of achievement with control groups of later entrants of similar abilities are made . . . the advantages of postponing early entrance to first grade programs as they are presently conducted are very real."

Many who insist on the ability of the very young child to read ridicule the statistics that suggest a relationship between early reading and the increasing number of children who are becoming disabled in learning. They say that educators simply make better diagnoses these days. Unquestionably, advances have been made in diagnosing children's problems. But it is impossible to ignore the impressive studies that indicate that learning problems become more frequent as children go to school earlier and earlier.

Helen Heffernan (65) of the California State Department of Education suggests that we may be making children more vulnerable to the pressures of our highly verbal society. Like many of the other researchers we have cited, she concludes that children who wait until they are older to go to school become better readers and more highly motivated learners than those who go to school earlier. Noting that ". . . there is a cultural pressure in our society to make every child learn to read in kindergarten or first grade," she suggests that we may be ". . . denying children their childhood by forcing formal language and reading on them at too early an age."

Dr. Heffernan (65) further points out that ". . . when children have difficulty in reading, parents blame the school and teachers blame the home for exerting undue pressure." But actually, a number of factors may be involved; the possibilities include hearing defects, visual defects, speech difficulty, cultural factors involving different languages, nutritional problems, inadequate rest, frequent family moves and therefore changes of school and home environment, chronic illness, physical handicap, unrecognized seizures and so on. She recommends wisely that perhaps we need to enlist the cooperation of pediatricians in trying to reverse the pressure for early schooling. She insists that those who know the least about their children tend to be those who are the most demanding of the school.

Dr. Frances Ilg and Dr. Louise Ames (75) conclude that it is "... probable that a large amount of the so-called 'reading disability' cases which are so unfortunately prevalent in our schools today come not from actual 'disability' on the part of the children who are failing their reading requirements in school . . ." but from the school's attempt to force unready children to perform at levels for which they are not prepared. Except in the Scandinavian countries, we have found that most preschools are geared, at least in part, to readying children for the basic learning skills. They provide convenient busy work for children who normally should be exploring on a wider basis for themselves.

Still another authority, a psychologist from the Catholic University of America, Washington, D.C., Hans Furth (47), reached similar conclusions. He warns:

> . . . Mark well these twin conditions: learn reading and forget your intellect. The average five- to nine-year-old child from any environment is unlikely, when busy with reading or writing, to engage his intellectual powers to any substantial degree. Neither the process of reading itself nor the comprehension of its easy content can be considered an activity well suited to developing the mind of the young child.

Educators will sometimes insist that their preschool, kindergarten or early grades involve no pressure to read. We believe, on the basis of recent investigation in several states and in Europe and the Orient, that this is not generally true. Halliwell (63) declares, "Any observer of a first-grade classroom would notice the large amount of class time devoted to the reading program. . . . Most first-grade teachers feel that the teaching of beginning reading is their most important goal."

Researchers in the area of mathematics have come to conclusions similar to those of reading researchers. Among the most prominent of the studies relating to arithmetic was that of Torsten Husén (74), Professor of International Education at the University of Stockholm who, in 1967, reported the results of an international study of mathematics achievement and attitudes toward school. His subjects were 13-year-olds in Australia, Belgium, England, Finland, France, Germany, Israel, Japan, Netherlands, Scotland, Sweden and the United States. Although Dr. Husén's research did not center on entrance age, University of California psychologist William Rohwer (123) examined Husén's data and found that the earlier a child had entered school, the more negative were his attitudes toward school. In Rohwer's words, "There is no indication in these results that revising the mandatory age of school entry to younger levels would improve the student's chances of subsequent in-school success.

While research provides ample reason for questioning laws that require early school entrance, it also raises the adjunct issue of placing girls and boys at the same maturity level. Lowell Burney Carter (26) of Austin, Texas, studied the achievements of boys and girls separately. He found that at the sixth-grade level, the older girls were significantly superior to the younger girls in reading, spelling and English, although there was no significant difference in arithmetic achievement between the two groups. Older sixth-grade boys were significantly superior to the younger boys in all four subjects. Chronological age was even more important to achievement with boys than with girls.

Rather sharp developmental differences appear between boys and girls during the early years. Nearly all of us have sat in schoolrooms where girls were generally considered to be brighter than boys. In most cases, it was assumed to be the natural thing, sometimes only grudgingly admitted and occasionally denied. Research, however, gives a clear picture of the basic reason for this difference.

Girls simply mature faster than boys. During the early years, girls are commonly six to nine months or more ahead of boys in maturity. So they are more nearly ready for school. Their superior early achievement is one of the clearest proofs of the importance of readiness in school. It also raises many questions. For example, why do most states set mandatory entrance ages at the same levels for both boys and girls? We can find no sound reason except expediency. If children were left out of school longer and the gap between the sexes were allowed to close, would it then be logical to have boys and girls of the same age in the same grades? We believe so. With less mature boys in the same classes with girls, should the boys be expected to behave as well? Not really, and the records largely prove that they do not. Should it be assumed that boys will be more frustrated and anxiety-ridden than girls and get into more trouble? Studies show that this is exactly what happens. A far greater percentage of boys than girls become delinquent during these years.

R. Vance Hall (61) conducted two studies on the relationship of the school-entrance age of boys and girls to school achievement. In his first study he found that 801 out of about 12,800 elementary school pupils had been retained or held back from progressing with their class-mates. Almost three-fourths of these were boys. And of those who were retained, about 78% of the boys and 80% of the girls were underage when they started the first grade. In another study, a random selection was made of 607 third-graders and 556 sixth-graders, of whom slightly more than half were underage at school entrance. When these children were given Science Research Associates (SRA) achievement tests, the underage children, especially boys, were found to achieve at a lower level in comparison with overage boys and girls.

In nearly all comparisons of reading skills of boys and girls of the same age, the results have significantly favored the girls. In a study of 16,000 British students conducted by British psychologist Ronald Davie and his colleagues (33), there was evidence that among boys and girls of the same age more boys than girls were reluctant to go to school and more boys than girls have temper tantrums. This study concluded that far more girls were happy at school than boys. We must conclude that maturity is a very important factor.

"The future of any society," Robert Hess (70) says, "lies in its ability to train, that is, to socialize its young." He calls on parents and educators of both boys and girls to demonstrate a sense of responsibility. On the basis of the facts presented here, this socialization will not be accomplished through sending children to school at an early age. Indeed, Louise Ames (117) warns, "School speed-up is senseless. If your child is having trouble in school, check his grade placement. Don't be fooled by his birthday age, I.Q. tests or early aptitude for reading. Send your child to school when he is ready—not before!"

10.

Comparing Home and School Costs

Harvard's Jerome Bruner (21) has been heralded widely for insisting that any subject may be taught to anybody at any age in some form. And while there is much truth to this theory, the conclusion does not point inescapably to a school situation. Nor does it establish the need nor desirability for formal learning of the 3-R's at home. Parents should realize that the young child will be educated from birth, whether he stays at home or goes to preschool or even a day-care center. Simply to be alive and awake is to be educated.

The basic question to be answered, then, is, what *kind* of education should we plan for the child, what kind of development most concerns us in his life? Is it possible, as some suggest, that simple at-home education is best? And what can we afford in term of both financial costs and risks to the child?

There is a feeling among many parents, educators and legislators that the nation can afford universal preschool and day care for its children, regardless of cost. This may sound promising to some, but it does not work out that way. In community after community, *handicapped* children now suffer for lack of funds. If we cannot pay even for adequate early care for the handicapped, how can we pay for preschool for everyone? According to *Wall Street Journal* reporter David Gumpert (60), frustrated and angered parents from coast to coast have initiated court suits asking state and local governments to supply the care for which the laws already provide. To finance early schooling or care for children who do not need it clearly means that less support will be available for those who do need it.

Recently, as we have noted, a few educators have begun stressing the need for early childhood professionals to work with the parents and their home, rather than with the children and schools. Some envision a sort of giant Home Start Program, with skilled teachers and aides working from house to house, or through community agencies. One advantage of this type of program is that it avoids a variety of expenses associated with the traditional preschool—building costs, bussing, and salaries for superintendents and supervisors.

While first consideration must always be given to the child's needs, common sense tells us that we must not be careless about the use of money lest we risk future programs. As it turns out, the research on home-and-parent projects suggests that financially they may be the most feasible. Impressive studies such as that previously cited by Harvard psychologist Sheldon White (153) and a recent report by Stanford Research Institute's Meredith Robinson (121), question the effectiveness of the recent large federal and state funding of early childhood experiments and programs which have promoted earlier schooling. Christopher Jencks (77), in his analysis of the widely acclaimed report by sociologist James Coleman of John Hopkins University on efforts toward providing equality of educational opportunity indicates that, in general, increased spending levels in schools have had relatively little impact on improvement of education.

While more research is needed on dollar costs of homing versus schooling, where facts are available, home programs have almost invariably been found to cost less than preschools or day care for comparable numbers of children. Experiments with home visitor programs conducted by Phyllis Levenstein (90), Susan Gray (57) and others proved these programs to be effective, practical, flexible and less expensive than out-of-home programs.

Specifically, expenses for a quality preschool program have been estimated at from $1,500 to $3,000 or more per child per year. One of the more successful of such programs, directed by University of Wisconsin psychologists Rick Heber and Howard Garber (64) for deprived Milwaukee children, costs about $5,000 yearly for each child. Among the most distinctive factors in Heber's program are a very small adult-child ratio and consistency of care —similar to that of mother and child at home.

As for home programs, the cost per child for home visitors was examined in a five-year study conducted at George Peabody University at Nashville, Tennessee, and reported by Christopher Barbrack and Della Horton (7). They found that the average yearly cost per child for one such successful program was less than $325.

While the figures may represent extremes in cost between preschool and home care, they do suggest that working with children in the home is usually much less expensive. A caution should be observed in comparing costs: The bases for comparison must be consistent. For example, a cost that includes schooling or day care plus comprehensive services (medical, psychological and others) should not be equated with a figure showing costs of schooling alone. Nor should whole-day schooling or care be costed against care for briefer periods. The neglect of this caution is one reason the research literature has often been confusing.

Early childhood researcher Earl Schaefer (131), who believes the home usually is more effective in promoting the child's intellectual growth than the preschool, suggests that teachers work once a week with parents of young children in the home, rather than bring the children into preschool situations. Dr. Schaefer adds, "A program that has trained parents to educate their children, as contrasted with a preschool program, has equal short-term effectiveness, has greater long-term effectiveness, is far less expensive." It also has the effect of diffusing its benefits to other children in the family and throughout the neighborhood. Instead of offering early schooling to all children, it is Dr. Schaefer's conviction that ". . . we should be offering all families training, methods, materials and consultation designed to support their work as educators." He calls for family-centered instead of child-centered programs.

Parenting specialist Dorothy Rich (119), working on a parttime basis and with little financial support, has set an example for community workers who may be interested in teaching parents how to teach their own children. She systematically conducts workshops and institutes for teachers, caregivers and parents in the Washington, D.C., area. In her Home and School Institute, she and her colleagues are continually at work developing materials whose aim is to build self-respect in homes and to join the home with the school in a community partnership in education. One of Mrs. Rich's mottoes is an old Chinese proverb, "A good parent is worth ten thousand schoolmasters." In a similar program in Benton Harbor, Michigan, Andrews University psychologist Dr. Conrad Reichert and community leader, Mrs. Helen Ford, train ghetto mothers to help other welfare mothers learn better the art of homemaking and effective parenting.

Even the idea of providing care for poor children so that their mothers might find jobs should be reexamined. As Finland's Annikki Suviranta (142) points out, the value of services in the home (including child care) has risen so sharply that women are well advised to evaluate costs and outcomes before taking outside employment. Dr. Meers (96), testifying on the 1971 Javits-Mondale proposal for wide-ranging child care, noted that day care—not to mention preschooling—is expensive if it is to be effective. He attributed the heavy turnover of day-care personnel in other countries to their less-than-competitive pay. He also pointed out that when the adult-to-child ratio goes up to eight or ten children to one caretaker, childhood distress increases astronomically. He suggested that ratios of even five children to one care person may result in depersonalization of the child, a failure in the development of the child's personality that is Dr. Meer's greatest concern in day care.

Dr. Benjamin Spock (140) presented the problem another way:

> Some mothers have to work to make a living. Usually their children turn out all right because some reasonably good arrangement is made for their care. But others grow up neglected and maladjusted. It would save money in the end if the Government paid a comfortable allowance to all mothers of young children who would otherwise be compelled to work. . . . It doesn't make sense to let mothers go to work making dresses in a factory or tapping typewriters

in an office, and have them pay other people to do a poorer job of bringing up their children.

Most cost estimates for child care include employment of a variety of caregivers, teachers and aides. The younger the children, the more demanding the job. The careperson must be mother, nurse, arbiter, nutritionist and playmate. Many early schooling advocates believe that somehow they will be able to find preschool teachers who combine the mother's concern and dedication with professional knowledge. But educational administrators know, from long experience and from a glance at their budgets, how difficult it is to find such teachers.

It is logical, then, that the parent, not the school, should be accountable for assuming the greatest responsibility for the welfare of his child. Part II of this book suggests how mothers and fathers can enjoy effective and responsible parenthood.

Part II

Introduction

Up to this point, our book has been focused on the major issues in early childhood education today. These are all related to the basic issue of whether a child's early education shall be centered in the family or in some more formalized program outside the home. We have explained the vital contributions made by the family to the growth and development of the young child, and have emphasized this with supporting evidence from current research. The inability of some families to provide the necessary home conditions for children's early learning experiences makes out-of-home child care an advisable alternative at times. But the home and family environment is always preferable if it can possibly meet the child's needs.

Whether at home or out of the home, a child will

learn. It is what he learns, how he learns and when he learns that have become crucial questions. Answers to these questions must, of course, be based on a sound knowledge of children's growth and development. Ignoring such knowledge, either deliberately or inadvertently, has caused much ECE confusion. Taking ECE out of the home has made it a major social and political football. The notion that children must learn basic academic skills before they are 8 years old has resulted in the trend toward earlier and earlier entrance into school. As we have shown, this indicates a real oversight of available knowledge about child development.

When parents begin to realize that their child's basic welfare is involved in ECE, they can take steps to insure the best possible programs for their children. In some instances, this may mean making their voices heard by their legislators. At other times, they can cooperate with their community or neighborhood so that home environments can be maintained for very young children. Hopefully, schools and other organizations will make plans for increased parent education in the future. And parents should be encouraged to take advantage of such opportunities.

The suggestions on child development offered in Part II of this book are working now and will continue to work. The degree of their success depends upon a family's willingness to adapt and to try to make them work for their child. Space limits the number of problems that can be treated. So the concern here is to deal with common childhood reactions in simple, constructive ways. Since no two children develop at the same rate, these chapters have been written with the assumption that there will be much overlapping. There may be, for example, *normal* or *typical* 1-year-olds, but there is no absolute standard of development for the child at age 1, only generalized approximations of behavior. In each age group, the child will be treated in at least four ways: (1) reactions that may be expected at this age level; (2) special needs of this age; (3) play things; and (4) activities and opportunities for learning.

Chapters 11 to 15 were written by the two authors from thirty-seven years of personal and clinical experience with young children, and from thirty years of consulting activity in North America, the Orient and Europe, variously as reading specialist, developmental psychologist, director of a cerebral palsy clinic, and as a teacher in or administrator of preschools and other schools at all levels. Insofar as practicable, this clinical experience was consistent with available ECE research and evidence from related fields. Finally, Part II is offered from a happy parenting experience by a mother and father who realize that there is still a great deal to learn.

11.

Birth to 18 Months

A baby's mental and physical growth from birth to eighteen months is spectacular. And the influence of his environment, even for the first few months, should never be underestimated. While his stages of development follow a general order common to all normal babies, each baby is different from every other in the timing and strength of his achievements. He cannot be hurried, but if his abilities are recognized, they can be expanded and improved by practice.

During the first year of his life, the baby grows faster than at any other time after his birth. He may double his weight within 4 or 5 months and triple it by age 1. Because of his particularly rapid growth during the early weeks, he sleeps most of the time. He is not much concerned with the outside world.

One of the baby's most dramatic early acts is the announcement of his birth—a lusty cry that both expands his lungs and fills its cells with air. This private performance will often be repeated during his first months—day or night. It may seem heartless to ignore the cry when the baby is released from loving arms and put to bed. Yet once all his basic needs have been cared for, responding to his every outcry encourages discontent and continuing demands for attention. It is one of the surest ways to rear a spoiled child.

Parents will do almost anything to insure their baby's happiness. Yet it is hard for them to wait patiently for normal developments. They often point proudly to the baby's first "smiles," which are usually only a reflex action. At about 6 to 8 weeks, however, the baby will smile in recognition of a friendly face. Before long, he will begin to coo, babble and even laugh aloud. Sometimes, he will speak several words by the end of his first year and often twenty or more by 18 months.

Shortly after birth the baby begins to become more and more active physically, waving his arms, pulling in and stretching his legs and clenching his little fists. For his size, he is surprisingly strong. He tightly grips your finger. He curls up his legs. If you attempt to extend them, he will try to pull you to him. Except for sucking and swallowing, the baby's first muscular movements are not planned, and they seem without purpose. But soon he is grabbing, grasping and putting things in his mouth. He will normally develop his hands and fingers before his legs.

By the age of 4 months, he is able to turn over. He can now hold up his head for short periods of time. By 8 months, he typically can sit up, creep and pull himself up to his feet, and soon he is standing alone. From 12 to 18 months, he begins to walk alone, and he steadily improves his balance. Do not be disturbed if he takes longer; many, even the brightest, do. If there is any serious question, see your baby's doctor.

Around 4 months of age, or later, depending on your doctor's instructions, the baby may begin to eat solid food. Before 12 months, he will be able to finger-feed himself. Then he will learn to eat with a spoon and drink from a cup. Undoubtedly he will be messy with his food. His small muscles, in this case his fingers, are not well coordinated, and, in fact, will not be for several years.

By 6 or 7 months, he will begin to cut teeth, and he will usually have 12 to 16 teeth by 18 months. During this time, his sleep needs drop from 18 to 20 hours per day down to 12 hours at night and a nap or two during the day.

REACTIONS THAT MAY BE EXPECTED

The new baby actually recognizes no one in his first few days of life. Around 2 or 3 months, however, he is responding happily to his parents, his brothers or sisters and a variety of things around him. He may cry or be disturbed by sudden movements, by loud sounds, by strangers or even strange objects. Yet, normally, he enjoys watching those around him.

He likes to be played with, warmly talked to and gently held. He loves the sound of friendly voices and is soothed by soft music. He finds special security with his parents, particularly with his mother.

From a very early age, he enjoys simple rhyming verses and being read to—even though, for years, he may not understand most of the meanings. Talking and reading at this age is a game for him—a game that means security and love. Physical closeness at story time, preferably on your lap, will be a treat to him for several years to come.

Gradually, he begins to imitate the actions, facial expressions and sounds, even the tones of voices of those around him. By the end of the first year, he may wave goodbye, throw a kiss, reach his arms to be taken or play peek-a-boo. He usually will be able to imitate several single-syllable sounds made by animals, birds, the clock. He also learns to play with simple toys, shaking a rattle or a bell, hitting a cup with a spoon, throwing large balls and putting one thing into another.

His senses of sight, sound, touch, taste, smell, are able to function, although they are not yet under responsible control. He hears, but often he does not completely understand the *why* of his parents' "no," until he reaches age 8 or later. At an earlier age, he must learn to obey simply because you say so. Often, before the end of his first year, he can obey, but may not for his memory is short, and he has not yet developed a conscience. He cannot be trusted out of your sight unless he is in his bed or playpen.

If a child has taken a forbidden object, by 11 or 12 months he usually will relinquish it upon request. If he remains reluctant, he may cooperate best when a box or basket is held out to him, since he likes to put things into a container. He will respond more cheerfully if you say "thank you" and smile as you hold out your hand or the container. Also, since he is easily distracted, he will usually accept a substitute object.

During this period, a baby should seldom, if ever, be spanked. A pat on his bottom or his hand may be necessary at times with a firm "No." But he should never be disciplined in anger. An impulsive slap in the face shows parental impatience or anger. And discipline seldom has the desired effect if the parent is not in control of his own emotions.

Fortunately, most parents manage to provide reasonably good physical care during the critical first year of the child's life. When their baby is helpless and new, parents pay close attention to his development and they often keep in touch with their doctor or baby clinic or refer to good books on baby care. After his first birthday, however, the baby often is neglected in this respect. Yet certain hazards to his health and safety increase as he becomes a mobile toddler. Furthermore, some parents become increasingly confused by his emotional outbursts and other signs of a developing personality. This is not the time to lower the acuity of parental attention—it is the time to provide activities and an environment that will help him grow in a balanced way—physically, mentally, emotionally and socially.

NEEDS OF THIS AGE

While some babies have better dispositions and some are healthier than others, generally babies are not born with bad habits and personalities. These are developed. In this respect, also, the baby's early weeks and months are of such importance. This is the time to establish physical health and emotional security as a basis for mental growth and the development of self-control.

Since the baby learns so well by imitation, a great responsibility rests upon the mother or her surrogate to help him to develop a happy, pleasant disposition. Generally, he will smile when she smiles and will otherwise react to her personality. Typically, the less she responds to his unnecessary crying, the less he will cry. The more happily she reacts to his pleasantries—cooing, smiling, babbling—the more he will learn to be pleasant.

The baby's greatest need is warm, loving, continuous care by one or two persons—his parents, if possible. The certainty of his parents' love is something a baby can feel in their patient and consistent care. He delights in their cuddling, holding, rocking and in their smiling conversation. He is especially secure if he can be nursed at his mother's breast, not only because of the unique health-protecting nourishment of her milk, but also because of the cooperative, loving intimacy that such nursing usually provides.

Yet love is not indulgent. The baby will rule the household if he is allowed to, but the parents' will must be dominant. It is a tragic mistake to allow children to have their own way in babyhood and hope to reason with them when they get older. Obedience and self-control must be taught early. To accomplish this goal, the parents also must be self-controlled. During the first few months of life, obedience is taught largely by regularity of schedule. It cannot be done by spanking or by reasoning. But regularity and consistency will create an atmosphere in which obedience will flourish.

As far as possible, the schedule should fit the baby and anticipate his needs. Within reason, his bath, nap, meals, playtime, outdoor period or exercise and bedtime should come at about the same time each day. Of course, the needs of the family as well as the baby should be considered in setting up a practical schedule.

Be careful about feeding on demand. "Demand feeding" developed as a reaction to the once-popular rigid, by-the-minute feeding routine, which virtually eliminated cuddling. But the idea of demand feeding was not generally intended to mean that the mother should feed at the baby's every cry. Somewhere in between these extremes, the mother can find a common-sense way to establish a schedule that is best both for her and for the baby.

The fact that mother's milk is more quickly and easily digested than cow's milk should be considered in setting up the schedule. Breast milk forms a fine, flaky curd in the baby's stomach that normally can be digested much more quickly and easily than the much larger, heavier curd of cow's milk.

The newborn baby usually requires food every three or four hours, depending upon his weight. It takes the stomach this much time to digest one feeding. If the infant cries sooner than this while receiving sufficient nourishment at each feeding, more food is not what he needs. Here is the first opportunity to begin to teach the child the basic principle that his wants can be delayed. A change of position, a drink of warm water or another distraction may quiet him.

Most children's eating problems can be prevented. The training in good eating habits begins when the infant is in his mother's arms. By feeding him at regular intervals and less frequently as he grows older, the child learns that he eats to live, rather than lives to eat. If he is not given sweets or overseasoned food, he will relish simple, healthful food. For this reason it is best to avoid butter on his vegetables, sweetened cereals and jam or jelly on his bread.

The food placed before the child either weakens or strengthens his physical health, which, in turn, affects both mental and moral health. Unless a child is on a special diet prescribed by a qualified physician, he should not eat anything between meals. The great American habit of snacking has come to be sacred in many households, but it threatens the child's health. If his diet is carefully planned in his early years, a lifetime foundation for good eating habits will have been laid.

A child should never be forced to eat. If he is well and the parent does not overload his dish, usually he will eat all he needs willingly. Since appetite varies from time to time, it is wise to serve small portions and add more. Sometimes, too much food on the plate is discouraging.

Often the child tires of feeding himself before the meal is over and needs help to finish.

The food should be carefully chosen and prepared. Unjustified complaints should not be permitted. Nor should he hear another member of the family express a dislike for a certain food, for he is a mimic. In such a case, unless the food is actually bad tasting, it may be necessary to give very small servings of one thing at a time in order of importance. But never force or show unusual concern. Otherwise the child may use poor eating habits to get attention.

If, for some reason other than illness, your child refuses a certain important food, recheck its quality and taste. If it is good, simply and quietly remove the food and let him wait until the next meal before allowing him to eat. Then serve a small portion of the same food again, giving him nothing else until that is finished. Natural appetite will usually take care of the problem. But if not, be patient and repeat the process at the next meal. Gentle persistence, without obvious pressure, is all that is normally needed. Overanxiety and indulgence on the part of the mother probably create most eating problems.

Small children need to learn to like new foods because good nutrition demands a varied diet. While children are not born with strong likes or dislikes, they do not always take readily to the taste and texture of new foods, especially vegetables. Therefore, the method of introducing new foods is important.

When the doctor says it is time to start solid foods other than cereal and fruit, try fluffy baked potato. It is nutritious, yet is not a great change from cereals. Mash it finely, moisten with a little milk and salt lightly. After the baby becomes accustomed to this, you can introduce him to other vegetables. For example, mix a teaspoonful of pureed carrots or green beans with the same amount of potato, then gradually substitute more of the vegetable until the baby has learned to like the new vegetable. The same method can be applied to new fruits by adding them to applesauce or mashed banana—fruits that babies usually accept willingly.

For a baby who has a very good appetite, simply offering a small bite or two of the new food at the beginning of the meal and then going on to the familiar food is often sufficient.

Sleeping problems can be prevented, too, by not letting bad habits become established. For instance, avoid putting a baby to bed with his bottle. As an inducement to sleep, it often appears to be a good solution to the bedtime problem, for it involves a simple operation and is convenient. But the baby becomes dependent on his bottle for sleep. Later, when he outgrows the bottle, there may be difficulty getting him to sleep without it.

The baby should be held until he finishes his bottle or is nursed from the breast. Then he should be put tenderly to bed and tucked in. This is a mother's way of saying, "It's bedtime. It's time to go to sleep." He then learns from the very first what being put into his bed means. And unless he is ill any crying or fussing should be ignored. Children who are handled in this way from the beginning are less likely to "fight" sleep later.

Thumb-sucking is another example of a habit that can be avoided by simple preventive measures. While often babies start to suck because they are hungry, overtired or simply bored, sucking eventually becomes necessary for a feeling of security. The habit is particularly troublesome because it may contribute to misshapen teeth.

To prevent thumb-sucking, first it is important to see that the baby is getting consistent loving and enough to eat. Since thumb-sucking often starts at bedtime, it is relatively simple to keep the baby from getting his thumb to his mouth by putting him in a sleeping bag or other sleep-wear that covers his hands. At first, this may frustrate him, and it may seem heartless. You may feel that it is simpler to let him go to sleep happy with his thumb in his mouth. But that is simply postponing a problem that will become more difficult. And the parent is using thumb-sucking as a crutch to keep the child quiet. Once good sleeping habits are established, restraint will no longer be necessary.

For the baby who is not breast-fed and who actually is deprived of enough sucking or who suffers unusually from colic, it may be that a limited use of the pacifier during the first three months will be the lesser of two evils. This, however, should be for an emergency period only, for dependence on "something in the mouth" during infancy may lead to the undesirable habit of always wanting to have something in the mouth in later years.

Physical activity is important to the infant. One of his happiest times is bath time, when he can move around and use his large muscles. He often giggles at the freedom to kick, stretch and squirm without the restriction of clothes. Encourage him to do this, raising his arms over-head and back and stretching and flexing his legs. He will enjoy being on his stomach, too, especially if his back is gently massaged. He must be watched if he is on a bed or table, for he can quickly wiggle off. After 3 months of age, he enjoys being on a clean sheet, or a blanket on the floor or in a playpen. Whenever practical, he should spend part of every day outdoors, dressed for the weather and pro-tected from danger.

Some older babies resent being laid down on their backs to be changed or dressed. However, conversation, laughter or funny noises will usually divert the child from the unpleasant interruption of his freedom.

During his first few years, the baby should not be lifted quickly or carelessly by his hands or forearms. Nor should he be swung, except with great tenderness. Certain tissues are not yet strong enough. Elbows of little children, in particular, can be easily dislocated. While this does not necessarily result in permanent damage, it is nearly always painful.

During this age period, the baby should be protected from small, sharp objects. Marbles, crayons and other small toys of older children can be dangerous if chewed or swallowed. And all drugs, cleaning solutions and other dangerous items should be so located that the youngster cannot possibly find them.

PLAYTHINGS

It is not necessary to buy expensive toys. In fact, most playthings can be made at home. But all toys should be of good quality and safe. Anytime after one month, the baby might begin to notice a bright toy tied to the side of his crib. Soon he will be attracted by a brightly colored cord or a cradle gym with dangling objects that he can reach. Toys in his crib will encourage him to play happily by himself when he awakes instead of immediately crying for attention or for food. When the baby's first teeth begin to appear, somewhere between six and ten months, he will need a solid rubber ring or other device to chew on.

As he grows, he will need such toys as smooth, unpainted wooden or plastic blocks, a soft ball or a washable, soft, stuffed animal or doll. (Animals and dolls should not have button-type eyes that can be removed and swallowed.) Firmly strung empty spools or very large buttons will add variety. He will love a cup and spoon with which to make noise, and a container into which he can drop things such as blocks, clothespins or other small, safe objects. When he is able to sit up for his bath, he will enjoy toys that float in the water.

When he begins to crawl, he should have the opportunity to explore, within limits, in a clean area. Such exploring provides a key educational opportunity. He also should have a low shelf or cabinet in the kitchen containing simple things that he can use while being close to his mother. The objects could include an old catalogue or magazine, some old pans with lids that fit, some empty cans that have had the sharp places smoothed and that will fit into one another and some nested measuring cups. Or give him empty plastic containers, boxes with lids and other safe, entertaining and constructive items.

If he attempts to get into your shelves or cabinets, gently but firmly say, "No, no," and move him near his toy cabinet. If he persists, quietly put him in his playpen. If you do not scold, slap or look angry, you will effectively teach him his limitations and the rights of others.

ACTIVITIES AND OPPORTUNITIES

Most "teaching" of the baby should take place incidentally, while caring for him, preparing meals for the family or doing routine housework. You cannot speed up the development of your child without great risk, but you can encourage and nurture his abilities. This is a matter of being aware of the learning possibilities of your child, then utilizing the daily activities to help him develop the senses by which he learns. As ancient Hebrew parents were instructed, "And you shall teach them diligently to your children, and shall talk to them when you sit in your house, and when you walk by the way, and when you lie down, and when you rise." (Deuteronomy 6:7)

Nevertheless, your baby should have a special time with you at least once or twice a day. It may be only five or ten minutes at first, but the time can increase as baby's attention span lengthens. It should be a time when he is pleasant and happy, not crying for attention. An especially good time is late in the afternoon, when often he will be restless and bored otherwise. Plan ahead and start before he begins to fuss.

Language development can be encouraged by responding to baby's babbling and by talking to him about what you are doing. Do not overwhelm him with chatter or nonsense but communicate in a simple, meaningful way what is happening. Use short sentences, correct names for objects or activities and clear, correct pronunciation. It is well to emphasize the main word, such as: "Now it is time for your *bath*," or "Shall we read a *book*?" He will learn to speak only as clearly and as well as you do.

Although there are many activities and opportunities for learning, the mother must not be so anxious to teach that she hovers over the child and directs everything he does. If he is to develop self-confidence, he needs to learn to be happy by himself and to do things independently as he grows older. You can encourage this independence even before he is 3 months old by putting him in his playpen several times a day during his short waking periods. If you do not have a playpen, improvise by laying chairs on their sides to form a pen in a clean, warm corner of the room.

If he becomes used to the playpen at this age, he will be prepared for other necessary limits that must be imposed in the months to come. He may learn to play in his playpen for as long as a half-hour at a time, two or three times a day. Besides developing independence, a good playpen provides a safe, clean area where the child can move about freely and develop his muscles in the process of learning to walk. The playpen should contain only one or two toys, seldom more, or he will be confused.

We suggest, however, that the playpen not be

overused. When you have time and can watch him closely, give your child the freedom of the house. He will learn faster and develop better. Even car seats, cribs and infant seats should not be allowed to interfere unduly with the freedom of the child, especially the freedom to be held and cuddled. While such items are often helpful, they should be used more for the safety and comfort of the child than for the convenience of the parents. In good weather, a protected place on the porch or outdoors will afford the baby much entertainment as he sees fluttering leaves and rays of sunlight and hears the sounds of birds or children playing and talking. And it is a good opportunity for distant vision, ophthalmologists and optometrists point out.

From birth, hearing is one of the things a baby can do best. He derives great pleasure from the soothing effect of soft, sweet singing by his mother, or recordings of lullabies, or a music box. Cuddling time, story time, bath time or bedtime are good times for quiet music. Livelier songs can be sung while you are changing him or otherwise caring for him. Songs such as "Here We Go Round the Mulberry Bush," can be adapted to any number of activities during the day:

This is the way we wash our hands,
Wash our hands, wash our hands.
This is the way we wash our hands
So early in the morning (before we start to eat).

There are a number of other enjoyable musical activities from which the baby can learn. Bounce him so that his feet touch your lap or the bed to the rhythm of a song. Or march around the room to music while carrying him. He can learn to clap his hands or play a toy instrument rhythmically while you sing or play the piano or a recording. If a pan and spoon are too noisy, make a drum from an oatmeal box, cymbals from small foil pie plates and rhythm sticks from half-inch dowels. A sealed plastic container containing dry rice or beans is a good homemade instrument to shake to the tune of the music. Don't worry if he does not keep time with your rhythms. Be happy that he is enjoying himself.

Some babies can enjoy "reading" books with mother as early as 9 months, if mother will make up a little song about each picture in the book, instead of just saying the rhyme or talking. Such songs may frequently be prefaced by a pointing game. For example, the mother (or father) asks, "Where is the apple?" She then points to a picture and answers her own question: "Here is the apple." Soon the child does the answering and pointing, making sounds and using inflections that resemble the sounds of the words.

The pointing exercise should not be too frequent or too prolonged. Continue only as long as the baby shows interest, perhaps only two or three minutes at first. Then repeat the same pictures and songs the next day before going on to any new ones. A small baby enjoys repetition. He loves the same things over and over, and he should have a little time to enjoy what he has already learned before going on to something new. Gradually, his attention span will lengthen to possibly five or ten minutes for that particular activity.

Often, the best type of book for this purpose is one you can easily make yourself. There should be only one simple, familiar item per page, such as an apple, a banana, a cat, a dog. These pictures should be clear, fairly large, colored and realistic. They can be drawn and colored or cut out of magazines, then pasted on pieces of heavy paper or cloth that are sewed or otherwise fastened together on one side.

It is normally better that the pictures not be exaggerated or absurd, such as cartoons or puppets. Children have so much to learn about the real things around them that they should not be confused with unreal things. Also, many children develop fears about imaginary creatures. More than one child has suffered from hearing about Little Red Riding Hood and the wolf. In fact, parents should be especially cautious about exposing small children to anything that may be frightening. This may be true, for example, of loud music with a heavy beat. It tends to make children nervous and irritable.

When the baby is as young as 3 months of age, you can start taking him on a daily tour around his room or the house, so that he can see and sometimes feel objects of various *sizes, shapes, colors* and *textures,* and hear their names. These objects may be toys, house plants, lights that you can turn on and off for his enjoyment, or the piano or record player, which makes interesting sounds. Let him look at and listen to a watch or clock; then, after waiting a few moments, say "Ticktock" to him.

Nearly every home has some pictures, books, decorations and personal items that the baby can safely touch, and others that are not his to play with. Now is the time to begin teaching which are which. If you are consistent, soon he will respond to your tone of voice when you tell him what he cannot touch, giving him a simple explanation; "This is mother's, I won't touch."

When the weather is pleasant, the baby tour can move outdoors—to hear and see the birds, to see, smell and touch the flowers, grass and leaves. He may crumple a dry leaf to hear the sound, or feel brick, cement, stones or sand. He should be allowed to watch and touch animals when it is possible. If there is an airplane or car in sight, point to it and name it, imitating the sound of the motor.

By 6 months or so you can show him in the mirror

where his eyes, nose, ears and mouth are, and tell him their names. Also show him where your eyes, nose, ears and mouth are, both in the mirror and on your face. Soon he will be able to point to his various facial features, as you ask him, for instance, "Where is your mouth?"

Sometimes, show him a mirror while he is eating a piece of bread or toast, so that he can see his teeth and tongue and how he chews. These are his first lessons in physiology and anatomy. Later, he can learn that the food he eats goes to his stomach, that he hears with his ears, sees with his eyes and smells with his nose. He should also gradually learn that good food, water, sleep and exercise make him grow strong and keep him well.

As you bathe the baby, you can teach him that parts of his body come in pairs. "Now we'll wash the other foot," or "Now we'll wash the other arm." Soon he can help wash his own knees, elbows or ears as you make a game of learning the parts of his body.

For the most part, home is the best place for a child during this period. Quietness, calmness and freedom from artificial excitement build strength in the immature, sensitive nervous system. It is important that the baby explore his immediate environment first. If there is no outdoor yard at home, a walk to a neighborhood park is a good substitute. But while special trips to the zoo, aquarium or farm are welcome, they are not necessary at this age. Too much visiting, too many trips to the supermarket at busy hours and other activities meant for older persons are overstimulating to small children and can make them nervous and high-strung.

12.

1 Year to Age 3

Physically your baby will grow at a slower rate from age 1 on, and he will generally eat less in proportion to his size. He may gain only three to six pounds in his second year. By the age of 2, he usually will be approximately half his adult height. He will begin to look less like a baby as he becomes more muscular, a result of his stepped-up activity. His body becomes larger in proportion to his head size, and his arms and legs become longer and stronger.

He still understands more than he can verbalize, but he will normally progress rapidly from a few words at 1 year to fluent speech by age 3.

He probably will be walking by 18 months, and perhaps even running. Both walking and running are on a broad base, with feet wide apart, to steady him. In spite of his small size, he can cover ground surprisingly fast. Little Columbus wants to explore everywhere; yet, he has little sense of direction and he is not yet able to turn sharp corners. He likes to push, pull, climb, drag, tug, lift and pound. "Perpetual motion" and "into everything" are descriptive terms for this age.

His eye-hand coordination continues to improve. He tries to feed himself but does better with fingers than with a spoon. His mouth is often the testing place for everything from blocks to rocks, as he tries to check out texture and taste. He may have all 20 of his first teeth by age 2.

He sleeps less now—about 14 hours including a daytime nap.

REACTIONS THAT MAY BE EXPECTED

At this period, the toddler is becoming independent. He wants to do many things for himself, yet he is often incapable of doing all he tries. For example, he wants to dress and undress himself. But while he can take off his clothes, he has a struggle trying to put them on, especially handling buttons or tying knots. Distinguishing the front of his undershirt from the back and the left shoe from the right are almost impossible problems.

When he cannot manage things he wants to do for himself, or when his language skill is not sufficient to express his wants, he becomes frustrated and sometimes angry. At this point he needs encouragement to do what he is able to do as well as patient help when necessary. If he still persists, and a tantrum results, it is wise to continue your activity as calmly as possible, completely ignoring the temper display. Slapping is never appropriate, but some tantrums may require his isolation with a remark such as, "You may stay in your room until you are through crying." In extreme cases, if the child becomes blue in the face or almost loses his breath in anger, the shock of an unexpected dash of cold water in the face may be necessary.

Since he is developing a sense of humor, he will respond to fun and games as long as you laugh with him instead of at him. The peek-a-boo game goes well with clothes that must go over the head; "Where is your hand (or foot)?" helps when putting on a sweater (or pants).

Though moving toward independence in some things, a child at this age is very dependent on his mother's companionship. He prefers her to anyone else and usually objects to being separated from her. He does not always react well to strangers, and it is wise not to force such acquaintances.

Some of his early fears of sudden movements or loud sounds may become less obvious as he grows older. Yet other fears may develop, depending on the example of the older individuals around him. Fears of the dark, of animals, of water and of imaginary creatures are often learned by exposure to pictures in books or on television, and people around him unconsciously pass on their own anxieties and apprehensions.

Many common fears can be prevented. The less varied or complex the environment, the better in general for the child of this age. He is not yet able to reason out why things happen, so he cannot anticipate events as you can. Therefore, you must anticipate them for him. For example, it is best to avoid sudden noises or actions around the toddler. And you can help him learn about the dark. You can, for example, take him out into the night to show him the stars to help him see that night is to be admired rather than feared.

The attention span of the child in his second and third year is short, but he can become surprisingly absorbed in something that interests him. You should note his interests, and help to increase his concentration by allowing him to have plenty of time to enjoy what he has learned. Moreover, let him repeat his activities, not only the first time, but also day after day. Repetition helps him develop better muscular coordination and increases his skill and speed of movement, as well as aiding his concentration.

By the time he is 2½, he has become a dawdler, spending long periods in handling, clasping and looking. Time means little or nothing to him, except for *now*. He does not understand yesterday, tomorrow or next week. He is not inclined to be hurried or delayed.

He plays side by side, or parallel, with other children, seeming to enjoy their presence. Yet he does not play well cooperatively and will not until he is at least 4 or 5 years old. Sharing usually means to him that he keeps the toy in question, in fact all his toys.

His most popular word is "no," but it may not always really mean "no." It would be wise to avoid asking questions or making requests that can be answered by "no." For example, instead of saying, "Wash your hands before lunch," say, "We will have lunch as soon as you wash your hands."

At 2½ to 3 years of age, the child is likely to be ritualistic. He wants to do the same things the same way day after day. Generally, this is a positive development, because it shows that he has learned the home routine well and is happy with the program. This period can be used to advantage in helping to establish habits of neatness and orderliness.

This is your opportunity to teach him how to fold his clothes neatly and to keep his drawers, closet, toys and other possessions in order. He will like to sort silverware as he puts it into the drawer. He can learn to set the table properly, in the process also learn sizes, shapes and numbers. He can help sort clothes both before and after laundering; so, he learns about colors and texture. He can put away groceries or sort nails and bolts with his father.

Don't let him become a prisoner of routine, however, to be so resistant to change that he becomes a dictator. He should never be allowed to create a major confrontation with you or to feel that he is your boss. It will be good for him occasionally to vary certain patterns. Have the other parent or his big brother or sister put him to bed occasionally, or have them assume some other responsibility in his schedule. Sometimes, have him wash his face *before* undressing, if that is not the usual routine. Such changes will help him learn that there is more than one way of doing things properly. The exceptions to this are regularity in the times for meals, nap, bed, or any routine that involves the body cycles of digestion and rest.

At this age, you should plan and prepare ahead of time if there is to be a major deviation in his program— a baby-sitter, a visitor or any change of location. As much as possible, he should know what to expect about changes that relate to him. It may take tact and some ingenuity, but the parent should always try to devise an approach that avoids a clash of wills.

NEEDS OF THIS AGE

At this age, consistent, warm, loving care still is the toddler's greatest need. It is infinitely better if this can be provided by parents instead of a substitute. The child of this age also needs guided freedom. Encourage him to be free in spirit. Yet, at the same time, help him to understand that certain rules are made for his protection as well as for the freedom and protection of others. It is entirely consistent that in order for a child to have such freedom, he must be given a track on which he can run, especially since he still finds security in routine. Lay down a few simple and well-made rules, then patiently and lovingly enforce them. You are laying the base for all his future behavior.

A child also needs to learn early in life to be cheerful and brave about small disappointments, hurts and troubles. You can help him by diverting him and encouraging him to pass lightly over his little discomforts. Don't pick him up every time he falls. You usually can tell the difference between a real cry of pain and one of selfish complaint. Your mature reaction will help him to develop strength of character. Give him loving sympathy when necessary, but not prolonged coddling or indulgence.

Don't shield him from difficulties. Rather, teach him to cope with difficulties according to his ability. Help him to learn that he may not always be able to do something the first time he tries, and encourage him to keep trying. In this way, he develops confidence in himself by finding out what he can do. It is possible that you will expect too much of your child, but it is more likely that you will not expect as much as he is actually capable of doing.

The toddler should not habitually be commanded or scolded. The parent should use simple statements and directions. Instead of "Johnny, put that down," say firmly, "That is not for Johnny." Expect to be obeyed. And *consistently* see that you are obeyed. Even though your child is very young, he can understand what is plainly told him. For this reason, the child needs to know the meaning of a quiet and firm "No." He should never be allowed to ignore it, even if you have to accompany it with a sharp slap on his hand. If he persists, remove him from the room or otherwise kindly but firmly see that he obeys. And be careful not to make "no" meaningless by overuse. If you are firm but also kind, loving and consistent, you can help your child establish the habit of obedience. The goal of discipline should be *self-discipline*. The best control is *self-control*, even at this early age.

The investment of a few years of your time to establish self-control in your child will pay big dividends later on. An indulged or disobedient child is neither a happy child nor a joy to his family or anyone else. With relief, his parents send him off to school as soon as possible, for he is selfish, exacting and unlovable. Worst of all, he is discontented with himself. He is insecure instead of self-respecting. Unfortunately, it is unlikely that he will care for school rules any more than home rules. There is evidence that such attitudes may lead him, ultimately, to disobey community and civil rules.

Obedience at this age is also important for the child's own *safety*. It will simplify your problems and provide a secure environment for his explorations, if you remove or lock up breakable or potentially dangerous objects and knickknacks. Unused light sockets should be taped, electric fans and heaters put away and gates installed at the head and foot of stairways. Provide a fenced-in yard for outside play. Or, where possible, take him to a park where he can run, climb and explore. Even with all these precautions, your youngster needs constant watching. He should be within sight and sound at all times. He cannot be held responsible for his own safety.

Children generally are found to have better all-around development when they are left to romp, as freely as practicable, around the house. Yet there are many times when the child must be placed in a playpen or other limited area. You will know that he has outgrown his playpen when he can climb over it. Then is the time for graduation to other limited quarters, such as a room with a gate across the door.

Establishing what your child can and cannot climb on may save you future embarrassment and keep your friends in a happy mood when you visit them. Parents who do not set limits ahead of time at home are seldom welcome visitors. No one enjoys witnessing your private war with your undisciplined child.

The toddler at this age cannot easily be hurried. This applies to routine activities as well as to his education. Take time to anticipate his activities for the day. If it will soon be time for lunch and he is busy playing, give him plenty of advance notice to put his toys away or to find a stopping place for his current project. Help with the finishing touches.

When cooperation is not forthcoming after you have given reasonable, clear directions, simply take him by the hand or carry him to the place where you want him to be. Do this without anger or scolding, talking of the next activity or distracting him with a toy. If it is a matter of changing clothes or getting dressed to go out, try to start far enough ahead of time so that there need not be any pressure or rushing involved. Within reason, he should be allowed time to do the things for himself that he wants to do. He should be given encouragement and instruction as he tries to be more independent.

The child's slowness in eating or dressing at this age can sometimes be exasperating to you. You may be tempted to nag and scold to hurry things up. But this will lead only to frustration on your part and very little improvement on his. If you want him to hurry, try to arrange circumstances so that his dawdling deprives him of his wants and privileges. The necessary pressure will be felt with less pain, and obedience should result.

If he dawdles at his meals, particularly between ages 2 and 3, be sure you do not put too much food on his plate. Remember that his appetite is less in proportion to his size than it once was. And managing the spoon-to-mouth operation can become tiring or frustrating to him. You may give him some help and encouragement by feeding him every other spoonful or the last few spoonfuls.

If none of this works, allow a reasonable amount of time—30 minutes or whatever time it takes for the other members of the family to finish. Then quietly and firmly, tell him that it is time to clear the table, and that he can finish the food in his plate at the next meal. His soggy cereal may be very unappetizing to you by the next mealtime; you may even feel that you are being cruel. But remember that his cereal also would be soggy if you allowed him to dawdle for another hour. And saving the food is more a logical consequence of his actions than punishment.

During these years, the toddler may wish to begin choosing his own foods. However, he is not yet capable of being a good judge. You should continue to give him small servings of balanced, healthful food. After he has finished what you have given him, he may be allowed a second helping of something he prefers. But he should not have more bread, milk or any other food until he has finished his first portions of the balanced meal you have set before him. Children have a tendency to fill up on some favorite food and neglect the rest. In general, simple foods are their favorites. They care less for casseroles and other food mixtures.

Many children will develop a pattern of becoming full before a certain type of food is finished. Our little girl had an excellent appetite, but for a few meals she left her tossed salad until last, then told us she was too full to eat it. Since it is not right to force a child to overeat, we simply changed the order in which we served our food. Thereafter, we served the salad first, not only to her but also to the rest of the family, until she learned to eat salads without complaint.

If there is a dessert, it certainly should not be served until the child has finished his basic balanced meal. Especially for small children with their developing teeth and bones, desserts preferably should be natural sweets, such as fresh fruit. On the rare occasions when an ordinary sweet dessert is served, the baby's helping should be kept small. Even a very small piece of pie or cake will often contain a fourth to a third of a child's total calories; yet, such sweets normally offer empty calories. They are high-energy foods without necessary natural vitamins and minerals, and as such they upset the nutritional balance in the child's meals.

If the proper groundwork has been laid in the first year, the child has already learned much about recognizing and respecting other people's property. Each member of the family should be protected from intrusion on his property, including the toddler. Every child should have a place for his own private possessions, even if it is only a cardboard carton in a corner that holds his toys. Ideally, he should have his own room, with a place for everything and everything in its place. But no matter what the circumstances, he can learn to take care of his own things best if he has some space, or even a box, that is entirely his own. And he should be taught to keep it orderly. When possible, each toy can have its own "house" or "garage." A chalk outline on a shelf or on the floor can mark the special place for each thing and make it more fun to put things away.

PLAYTHINGS

A child at 1 to 3 years especially loves push-and-pull toys. He will also enjoy a large ball, stuffed animals, soft dolls low steps and strong boxes to climb on and a pegboard with large pegs.

A child should have simple items that give him the joy of creating. A shoe box or a slightly larger grocery box leaves more room for the imagination than a manufactured toy. It can be used for a dollbed, a house, a truck to push or, with a string attached, a wagon to pull. The same is true of wooden blocks. It is surprising how a toddler can make them into a tower, a house or barn, a fence or a train.

There are few toys that will delight a child as much or as long as a simple sandbox supplied with a pail and a shovel, or with a few smooth, safe cans and an old spoon. He can spend much time digging tunnels, making roads, building mounds or filling the cans and pouring sand from one to the other. The sandbox can be either inside or outside the house. In cold weather or in an apartment, it can be kept in the corner of the kitchen. And you can use kitty litter, which is easier to clean up than sand. If you don't have a wooden sandbox, use a small plastic pool or tub. And in hot weather, when the sandbox can be outdoors, put a shallow tub or bucket of water near it.

At this age, there are times when both you and your child will profit from independent activity. It is important to teach your child that he must learn to amuse himself some of the time. Provide a place within sight and sound of you, and provide simple toys that challenge his ingenuity and skills. He then can be busy and happy for some time.

It may be that your 18-month-old child can learn to assemble simple jigsaw puzzles, beginning with three pieces. These puzzles can be made at home: a simple, uncluttered picture of a familiar object or animal is mounted on cardboard or a smooth slab of wood, then cut into three differently shaped pieces that fit together well. Increase the puzzles to ten or more pieces by age 3.

You can add plastic jars with screw caps to his kitchen cupboard, and a shoe or cigar box with some discarded greeting cards inside. If you can find an old alarm clock with an unbreakable face, he will enjoy hearing it tick, and he will learn about cause and effect as he makes the bell ring. Large bean bags made of sturdy, firmly stitched material are good for stacking, throwing and catching. As your child grows older, he will enjoy trying to toss them into a container.

Indoor equipment for physical exercise when weather is bad could include an old mattress for jumping from a chair or box, or for turning somersaults. A small ladder laid on the floor next to the wall so that the toddler can walk between the rungs will help him develop balance. If the ladder can be placed safely and securely, it also can be used for climbing.

As early as 15 months the baby will enjoy playdough, which you can make with ingredients from your cupboard. Sift or mix well two cups of flour and one tablespoon of cornstarch and set aside. And ½ cup of salt and plenty of vegetable coloring to ¼ cup of warm water. When the salt is completely dissolved, gradually combine the two mixtures, kneading until it is of claylike consistency. Add more flour or more water if it is either too wet or too dry.

Let the child start with a piece of dough about three inches in diameter, but don't be disappointed if he does not make creative things. He is more likely to make shapes like pancakes, rolls and balls. Or at first, he may simply pat, pinch or fold the dough. When he seems to have experimented enough, the dough can be stored in a covered container in your refrigerator to be used again and again. To protect his clothes, put an old shirt on him backward. Because children enjoy mud as much as they do playdough, every child also should have the privilege of making mud pies when it is practicable.

It is sometimes difficult for parents to restrain their own desires for toys that are too advanced for the small child. A kite, an electric train, a dress-up doll with a variety of fashionable clothes or a coloring book with small crayons is not usually appropriate at this stage in his development, and will only frustrate him. Let him set the pace and play at his own level. Try to keep things simple.

Crayons large enough to be grasped in the fist can be provided at about 18 months, with sheets of paper large enough to allow the child free arm movements. Wrapping paper or unfolded grocery sacks serve the purpose. Do not expect anything but scribbling at first. Be careful not to discourage him, even though you may not be able to recognize any of his pictures until he is 3 or 4 years old. It is probably safer to say, "Tell me about your picture" than to run the risk of a seriously wrong guess. Compliment him for his effort, if not his genius.

ACTIVITIES AND OPPORTUNITIES

The goal for each child is that he grow in a balanced way —physically, mentally, socially, emotionally and spiritually. Most of the activities and opportunities suggested here are designed to bring together at least two or more of these objectives. Some are accomplished as incidental parts of the family's daily routine, while others are reserved for the precious daily time set aside for you and your child alone.

The child's play is important in his development. As a matter of fact, play for the small child *is* his work—a means of achieving better and better skills to do the things he sees older children and adults do. Conversely, his chores are often his play. In his world, there is no difference. He wants more and more to do what you do. Allow him to "work" when he is willing, even if he is inexperienced, clumsy and unskilled. Patience on your part now means that he is more likely to continue to be willing when he becomes more able.

Whether boy or girl, the young child of 2 and 3 loves to be his mother's helper. Make him feel that he is needed to help you in your daily household routine. Let him bring things from other parts of the house for you. Give him simple, one-step requests, such as, "Please get my shoes," or "Please bring Daddy's paper." Always thank him for his help. He can dust, wash and dry dishes, help set the table, help sort and put away clothes. He can sweep the porch with his little broom. Cut down one of your old brooms to his size if you can't find one his size, or nail a whisk broom onto a spare handle. Help him to identify his clothes and those of other members of the family, matching pairs of socks and learning where things go. He can help you make beds, patting the bed or fluffing the pillows.

All this should be done *with* you. At first, it will take more time and more patience than doing it yourself. But this is the best preschool education your child can have. As he learns to perform first simple, then more complicated tasks, he grows in self-confidence and emotional stability as well as in self-control. These are effective bases for his development as a social creature and as a citizen.

Toddlers especially enjoy having a special time with their father every day. Boys and girls can help their father polish or wash the car, clean the garage or put out the trash. Balls begin to be special fun at this age. The toddler and his father can begin by rolling the ball back and forth to each other. The child will become better and better coordinated and will be able to throw the ball in a few months, although catching a ball may take him longer. A bean bag is even easier to catch at early ages.

The toddler loves simple games such as hide-and-seek. He also likes pretending he is driving the car, with his own toy steering wheel fastened to his car seat. Make sure that he is securely fastened in his own seat, from which, without danger, he can see what is going on outside the car. He should never be free in the front seat, even with the car stopped.

A parent often enjoys a little rough-and-tumble play with his child. He can teach the child balance and, by age 2, how to do a somersault. Or they can pretend that both are animals, walking on their hands and knees on the floor and making the noises of the animal they are pretending to be. When he is able to run, your child will like being chased and will like to chase you. It is important that such active play not continue so long that the child becomes overexcited. And it is better that such activity not take place just before bedtime. Instead, he needs a story hour or other quiet time before going to bed.

The toddler's desire to do things for himself should be satisfied and encouraged. Give him finger foods to eat— crisp, whole-grain toast, wheat crackers, bite-size dry cereal or bite-size pieces of fresh fruits such as bananas, pears, peaches or apples. Teach him to chew thoroughly. Even some vegetable pieces, raw or cooked, can be handled as neatly with the fingers as with the spoon. As he becomes able, show him how to use his spoon for appropriate foods.

By now, he should help dress and undress and bathe himself. This is a good time for him to begin learning the names and functions of the parts of the body. Help him to identify the same parts on you, or on his doll or on animals. In connection with these activities, he should learn how to find his clean clothes and to keep his dresser drawers neat. He should be helped to hang his clothes on hooks and his towels on rods set at his height.

Shortly after age 2, he can wash his own hands and brush his teeth. He can also put away his toys in his own special place—box, or drawer or shelf—although he may need help at times.

Help your child develop his senses. You can teach

him to smell by showing him how you smell and by using things that have definable scents—flowers, foods and perfume. Point out the different colors, sizes and shapes of flowers and leaves. Provide opportunities to see animals, fish and birds whenever possible. Talk about them. Mimic their sounds. He can begin to learn animal names, what they say, and something about them. Make up little rhymes and a tune to go with them if you can

> *The little dog says, "Bow-wow-wow."*
> *That's all that he can say.*
> *The little dog says, "Bow-wow-wow."*
> *He talks to me that way.*

Substitute names and sounds of different animals.

When he is about 18 months old he will begin to enjoy a homemade scrapbook containing pieces of different textured materials for him to feel. The materials can include sandpaper, silk, satin, wool, fur, velvet, corduroy, cotton, smooth leather, suede leather, plastic, felt. Vary the colors if possible.

The child who lives in the country or on a farm can be close to nature easily. Yet parents who are alert to the child's needs can create reasonable substitute experiences. Books about nature and some nature programs on television can further help the child learn about the world around him.

The learning possibilities through music are almost limitless for the young child, and there are numerous ways you can introduce him to rhythm and melody. You can provide little objects like bells for you and your toddler to move while singing a song, and you can teach him to clap his hands to appropriate songs. You can make up songs about familiar objects like a clock, to which you move your arms in ticktock motion or click your tongue.

You may have a little problem at first when your child does not want to let go of the bell or other object when the song has been sung several times and it is time to go on to another activity. But if you simply hold out your hand and say, "Please," he usually will give it up. Always say "Thank you" when he does it. Then perhaps, you can give him something else to hold. Your example—whether it be manners or anything else—continues to be his most effective teacher.

Reading time is not just for amusement and entertainment at this age though it may provide both. Every activity is a learning session, and contrary to common practice, this is no time for absurd, fantastic tales. The child's power of concentration should not be wasted on make-believe stories when there is so much in the real world that he needs to know. True stories of nature, especially about animals and their babies, or stories from everyday life will be a delight as well as an educational experience for him. Stories about himself and about his own body and how it works often intrigue him. Read slowly, clearly and with expression.

This is also the beginning of the questioning age, which gives parents a great opportunity to satisfy the expanding curiosity of the child. Answer his questions as best you can. If you do not know the answer and have the time at the moment, look in an encyclopedia or other reference book with the remark, "Let's see what the book says." In this way, the child will learn that we can find out things we want to know from books. He will learn to look forward to the day when he can find out things from books.

Be careful about getting involved in a continuing series of questions that he may ask just to get attention. Avoid his interminable "why's" and "how's." It may be true that he needs to have your attention and some conversation with you, but when he asks questions that he can answer himself, it is often wiser and more fun to turn the questions back to him with "What do *you* think?" or *"You* tell me."

Another kind of pleasant learning game to play with your toddler is to let him watch you put a toy in a small box with a lid. Then you put the small box into a larger box with a closed lid and let him try to find the toy. After he has repeated the game several times, you can add a third box.

Another game is to put a small toy into one end of a tube such as the empty roll from a package of paper towels or toilet tissue. Then show him how you can use a stick to push the toy out the other end. See if he can do it. For him, it is a game full of wonder—and coordination. Later you can use a longer tube such as the ones that calendars come in. A homemade wire frame can be used to blow soap bubbles and catch them. Your child will enjoy the floating bubbles and can be shown the colors of the rainbow reflected from the light. As you become involved in these games, you will think of many others.

A variety of simple activities will help your child develop his senses and learn to use his muscles in better coordination. And in the process you will be giving him the finest basic education.

13.

Age 2½ to Age 5

From age 2½ on, the child's physical growth slows even more. But your child's growth in other areas is becoming more striking. His physical skills are developing, although still at an uneven rate. Coordination of his large muscles will improve considerably in this period. His small muscles and eye-hand coordination seem to develop rapidly. He will learn to button his clothes more easily and even to tie his shoes. At age 5, his head is nearing full size.

The 3-year-old has a lot of energy and seems constantly on the go. He is becoming quite steady on his feet. He can run, jump and climb. He can now turn corners and stop abruptly. He even alternates feet going up stairs instead of using both feet on each stair, and he probably jumps off the bottom step coming down. In another year or less, he will alternate feet going downstairs also. He is able to manage a tricycle, using the pedals to propel himself both forward and backward. At age 3, he can stand on one foot; at age 4, he can hop on one foot; at age 5, he can skip.

The experimentation and practice of the last couple of years have now made him quite adept at feeding himself and getting dressed. He will be more efficient at this if he has clothes that are simple and easy to manage, and if you lay out his clothes in the order in which he will put them on.

He can probably do a good job of washing his hands, and he also can be quite independent about taking his own bath, although he may need help with the finishing touches.

By the age of 3, he will normally have a full set of temporary teeth.

For the best of health, he still needs close to 12 hours sleep at night. And a short midmorning rest and an afternoon nap are still good ideas.

REACTIONS THAT MAY BE EXPECTED

At this age, your child is even more anxious for your approval. He also wants to be liked by other adults around him. If you have been firm, loving and consistent about his restraints and limits, he will grow increasingly cooperative during this period. On the other hand, if you confuse him by letting him get away with something one time but punishing him the next, he will not know what you expect of him. He will be unable to draw the line between acceptable and unacceptable behavior.

You will become exasperated if you expect your child to make valid choices before he is 3 years old, for he will either choose both alternatives or simply insist on having his own way. When he is about 3, he will enjoy making a choice between two familiar and acceptable alternatives, such as a trip to the market or to the park. However, he is not yet capable of making choices between acceptable and unacceptable behavior.

The secret of success here is in presenting the choice in a way that will prevent a negative reaction. For instance, do not ask, "Would you like to play outside now?" Rather, ask a leading question: "Would you like to ride your tricycle or play in the sandpile?" Or, "Do you want to wear your sandals or go barefoot when you play in the sandpile?" When it is bedtime, do not ask if he wants to go to bed, but assume that he is going to bed. A good question might be, "Do you want to take teddy bear or your dolly to bed with you tonight?" Or, "Do you want to wear your blue pajamas or your red ones?" When it is time to wash hands, you show what you expect him to do by asking, "Do you want to wash your hands with the white soap or the blue soap?"

In most instances, given this type of choice, you will receive much better cooperation from your child. And you will be helping him to learn to make decisions, though very small, which, in turn, will contribute to his growth in self-reliance.

By the time he is 4 or 5, he is showing the beginnings of the ability to reason. If you have given him the right background, he also can begin to make choices between acceptable and unacceptable behavior. Here are several examples:

1. Once he can understand that to keep well, we need to eat different vegetables, he will enjoy helping in the weekly selection of vegetables at the market. Or, he can help choose the vegetables you will eat at a particular dinner. During gardening season, he can even grow and harvest vegetables of his choice.

2. Once he can understand that his stomach needs

several hours to digest his regular meal and then needs to rest before eating another meal, he will be more likely to decide to save a cookie for after his lunch or dinner instead of eating it as a snack between meals.

3. If he has been shown by example and through stories that he should do to others what he would like to have them do to him, he will learn to share his toys with visitors. And he will take better care of other children's toys when he visits them.

The ultimate goal of behavior is self-control, self-discipline. We do not prepare our children for the realities of life when we are always telling them what to do and what not to do. Rather, we should allow them to use their own judgment more as they grow older, remembering, however, to keep their choices within the limits of their abilities.

During this period, your child will learn to play cooperatively with other children. He will begin to make friends, and around 4 or 5, he can begin to share and take turns. Boys' and girls' interests are still much the same at this time, and they play well together. Children playing together should be closely supervised; yet, they should have a minimum of interference. Unless there is a serious problem, it is better for them to solve their quarrels in their own ways.

Parents often are shocked to find that their small children are involved in sex play with their friends. If this happens, you should not be shocked, but should simply know where they are and what they are doing at all times. And begin early to explain the body functions.

Since a child is so impressionable, you should keep a check on the kind of companions he has. Do not assume that all his small friends are innocent of bad habits, rude manners, or deceit—things that children quickly and surely learn from one other. It is wise to avoid playmates who have been poorly trained or influenced.

Problems of association are among the most serious, but seldom recognized, dangers of care out of the home or in a nursery school. When your child is cared for by others, he is introduced to a variety of circumstances and influences over which you have little or no control. If some out-of-home care is necessary, you would be wise to select the day-care home or center with this in mind. At the same time, it must be observed that some preschools may provide a more favorable climate than many homes.

What a child sees and hears in his early years is imprinted deeply in his mind. You are ultimately responsible for what these things shall be. Do not feel that your child automatically will become more sociable and better able to get along with others because you place him daily in a group of children or provide him with many playmates. On the contrary, he will probably become more stable and better adjusted socially if he stays at home with you and shares the type of practical, everyday activities suggested in this book.

It also should be remembered that the young child is not yet able to handle competition, including the kind he faces in preschool. Some parents ask whether preschool competition is any different from the competition in large families. But being a member of a large family is different, because normally family members help and encourage one another.

However, groups of children in a typical nursery or day-care center must compete not only for toys but for the teacher's attention, permission and approval. There can be as many as twenty or more children for each adult. And mini-rivalries are often created. Teachers may ignore them as a matter of policy and practice, but they take their toll. Your child cannot tell you why he cries out in his sleep, or stutters, or sucks his thumb, or wets his pants or masturbates. But often these problems are symptoms of pressures too great for him to handle.

No matter how well trained, conscientious or skillful a preschool teacher may be, she can never have as deep an attachment or interest in a child as a wise, loving parent. Nor can she normally give the attention to the child that a parent can, even if the parent has several other children. Psychologists and psychiatrists generally agree that no one can fully provide a substitute for the tender, loving care of a good parent.

During this period, your child begins to sense a great deal of what goes on around him. He still may not understand the *whys* of things, but he sees *what* is going on. There is very little that is said or done that escapes his attention. For example, he may not comprehend the actual words you say; yet, he will get an overall impression from your tone of voice and facial expressions. He will note your conversations at the dinner table. He will observe your behavior when visitors come. Even your casual comments may be full of meaning to him. Thus he begins to form lifelong attitudes about race, religion, government, education and even politics.

Because he is an imitator, you will find yourself reflected in his language, manners, tastes and habits. There is really nothing that you can do without expecting him to try to do the same. If you smoke or drink, he may want to. When you take pills, he figures they are for him, too. He will copy the quality of your voice and the mannerisms of your speech.

You may feel sometimes that it is too much trouble to provide a sound example in all things. Yet this is the price of parenthood. For instance, you can learn to like foods that are good for you and your child. You can leave off the sugar on your cereal, stop eating between meals and even quit smoking. Your rewards will be better health and a better example for your child. If you learn to avoid angry words and control your speech and manners, you will have a better-controlled child. The challenge of a child should make parents better people. This is part of the miracle and blessing of their birth.

Most children from ages 3 to 5 exhibit a rapidly developing imagination. They like to dress up in costumes and pretend to be someone else. They will even imitate a bird, or fish or an animal. Some will invent an imaginary friend or pet, possibly to satisfy some inner need. During a few weeks' stay at a vacation cabin, our 4-year-old invented a snake named Bluey, who "lived" under our cabin. Every day, she fed him grass and leaves and provided fresh water. Sometimes, she would push special treats for him down an open knothole in the wooden floor. We went along with her, neither encouraging nor discouraging her. Before we left for home, she told us that "there really wasn't any snake called Bluey. It was just make-believe."

Because there is such a narrow margin between reality and imagination in the mind of your child, it is important that you treat his imagination with respect. If he reels off a tall tale, do not ridicule him or call the story a lie. If anything, it should be labeled "pretending." Or if you can joke with him about it, say, "You must have been dreaming." This will help him to distinguish between the real and the imaginary.

The child's ability to pretend may be valuable at times. On a short family trip, we failed to bring one of our little girl's stuffed toys for her to sleep with. So we took a big handkerchief, folded it in half and rolled each end toward the middle. Then we tied a big knot at the top and marked eyes, nose and mouth with a pencil. She hugged her new "doll" and went happily to sleep.

NEEDS OF THIS AGE

Because of your child's desire to experiment, you will need to supervise him carefully at this age. He gets into trouble easily. Continue your earlier practice of removing possible hazards from his play areas and locking up all matches, poisons and dangerous equipment.

If your youngster has been taught to obey, he will abide by such limits as, "You can ride just to the corner on your tricycle," or "You can go out as long as you stay in the yard." He will not reach the age of adequate reason until he reaches his integrated maturity level (IML) at anywhere from 8 to 11 years of age, so he has little judgment of danger. It is often wise actually to show him, even drill him, how not to run out into the street after a ball and to watch for cars in driveways. He can be taught how to cross the street, how to use tools, including blunt-end scissors, safely, and how to get a good footing and handhold when climbing. This may take repeated demonstrations and conversations *until a concern for safety* becomes part of his nature.

Continued security in your love and affection is the greatest single asset your child can have at this age. In large part, you show him that you care by consistency in your treatment of him and your management of his behavior. All your dealings with him should demonstrate to him that the rules of your home are just and reasonable. He should begin to understand that freedom is safeguarded by laws, and that his freedom ends where that of others begins. He must learn that disobedience to family rules leads eventually to serious problems and unhappiness for all concerned. Respect for authority and for property—his own and others—is thus an important part of what you will continue to teach your child. If you have shown respect for him, and if, in turn, you have earned his respect and provided an example of respect for those in authority—the traffic officer, the mayor, the president—he will imitate you. A child usually lives up to what is expected of him. With the proper parental encouragement, the child will try hard to do right or to be right.

Even though you are naturally and justifiably proud of your child, you will be doing him a disservice if you put him on exhibition before visitors to show off his cleverness. It is seldom wise to discuss his clever behavior in his hearing. This common practice tends to give him more notice and praise than he is able to bear. He may become forward, bold and impertinent, or he may withdraw or react in some other unattractive way. This is especially true if more than simple appreciation is shown, especially for things he should be expected to do. *As far as possible he should be allowed to maintain the simplicity and innocence of childhood without unnecessary pressures.*

It is tempting to omit the daytime nap now, especially since your child has more interests that keep him busy longer and since he fights it. You may feel that it is not worth the struggle. But at this age, he tires easily. He becomes irritable and restless. Often when the daytime nap is omitted, he is too tired to sleep well at night. If he continues his daily naps, he can then be permitted to stay up a bit later at night, giving the child more time with his father. Occasionally, a child may complain that he cannot go to sleep, even though you know he is tired. We devised a solution that went like this: "If you lie real still and keep your eyes closed for fifteen minutes, you can get up." Almost always, at the end of 15 minutes our child was sound asleep.

The food guidelines presented in the previous chapter still apply at this age for a balanced, healthful diet. The child's schedule should normally allow several hours between meals and no more than three meals each day.

Snacks are unwise. They are usually high in calories and low in food value. They tend to slacken the appetite for regular meals, slow digestion, overwork the stomach, deprive the body of needed vitamins and minerals, and frequently increase the total caloric intake beyond what is really needed, often laying the groundwork for obesity. Don't panic when your child says he is hungry, before it is mealtime. He will relish his food more when mealtime comes. A glass of cool (not iced) water between meals staves off hunger and is also an excellent tonic for the system. It is better for the child's evening rest if breakfast or the noon meal is the main or hearty meal of the day and the evening meal is kept light. Fruit, especially fresh fruit, and whole-grain toast or cereal are digested more quickly than vegetables and meat.

As the child moves toward the age of reason, consistency and patience are of increasing importance. Most problems that arise are brought on by such things as irregularity of routine, overstimulation—as by stereo, radio or television—and pressure to make your child do things beyond his ability. Overexcitement and crowds can also create problems, so the time spent at such amusements as the circus and the fair should be sharply limited in the small child's experience.

PLAYTHINGS

Because of his imaginative bent and his unbounded energy, the child makes excellent use of play equipment during this age period. He needs vigorous outdoor activity and plenty of opportunity to develop his large muscles. If you live in the suburbs or a rural area, he may have fences and small trees to climb. If you are an apartment dweller, he should have almost daily visits to the neighborhood park or playground where there will be a jungle gym or other equipment—to climb or slide down, or swing or teeter-totter on safely.

At home, even a small yard or porch can be inexpensively equipped with a sandbox, a safe ladder to climb or a small swing securely fastened to a strong beam. There are times when your child should be allowed the luxury of wading in mud puddles and making mud pies. In warm weather, wearing only a minimum of old washable clothes, he can find marvelous possibilities playing with sand or mud. He will not only build things—but will work out some of his own frustrations as well. Different-sized packing boxes, checked carefully for strength and to make sure there are no nails or slivers, can be great fun at this age. The child may pretend that any one of the boxes is a tent, a cave, a car, a plane or even a lunar module. He may use several of the boxes as different rooms of a house, a castle or a store. Or he may arrange them as tunnels, where he will crawl with delight. In addition to the boxes, a variety of lightweight boards are good for building and climbing.

Since boys and girls like to imitate the adult world, they like housekeeping toys and things for playing store. They also enjoy dressing up in clothes that help them pretend. Our little boy especially loved hats. He loved to play the part of a fireman, sailor, painter, farmer or chef, with only the appropriate hat on his head. Sometimes, the hats themselves were pretend, with perhaps a label or a badge to identify them.

Children enjoy hammering nails and making objects out of wood if they have the right equipment. At first, some parents prefer to buy or make a pegboard, so the child can practice with a wooden hammer and pegs. As he develops coordination, he can graduate to a steel hammer, preferably with a short handle and a broad head, and to wide-headed roofing nails. The saw he uses should be short and wide, and the wood should be soft enough for a small child to work easily. He can work on a portable work table with a small vise, which can be used outdoors in good weather and indoors at other times. He will learn to make many things. A block with a stick nailed to it may be an airplane or a boat, but before long, you may see him building reasonable-looking airplanes and a variety of boats that he can float in the sink, or a tub.

At this age one of the best materials for self-expression is finger paint. It can be made by boiling cornstarch to a thick paste and adding vegetable coloring. Your toddler may spread it with his hands, his arms, even his elbows. He can work on almost any kind of paper, although damp, glazed paper is best. Watch as he creates and erases many designs. After his completed picture is dry, hang it up on a wall or bulletin board.

Poster paints may provide another outlet for his creativity. Use large sheets of paper (newsprint, wrapping paper, the blank side of wallpaper remnants or even grocery sacks cut open). Almost any brush will do, but remember his hands have difficulty with small handles. You can make brushes by simply taping or tying little balls of old cloth or pieces of sponge to a stick or a spoon. Use washable paints. He should start with only one or two colors until he understands that each brush must be dipped in its own jar of paint in order to get clear colors.

It is best if he can do his work on an easel, which you can construct inexpensively. Take two pieces of plywood and hinge them together at the top, or use the sides of a large cardboard box "hinged" at the box corner. Set this up on any table or chair or on separate legs. Then attach a shelf or box to the lower edge of the easel, or fold out the cardboard, to hold the jars of paint. To protect the floor, place a piece of plastic or newspaper under the easel. Let your child use an old short-sleeved shirt, put on backward, for a smock.

In addition to paints, your child will enjoy large crayons, clay, paste and blunt scissors, along with colored paper, magazines or cloth to fold and cut. He can make a collage by pasting pictures from magazines or pieces of colored paper or cloth on a sheet of paper to form a design. Do not give him instructions about what to paint, and don't expect him to produce any particular thing. What matters is that he enjoy his play and that he create.

Because his attention span is increasing, even such simple activities as lacing or unlacing shoes can provide a fascinating, creative interlude for him. And such exercises help develop his small muscles.

With the array of equipment normally used by the active young child, it would be easy to allow the house and yard to be in a continual clutter. This clutter, however, could become a source of irritation to you and the rest of the family. And it is not good training for your child. He should be taught to pick up and put away as he goes along. Within reason, materials from one activity should be cleared up before another activity is started. Here again, example is the best teacher.

ACTIVITIES AND OPPORTUNITIES

Your child's attitude toward learning will reflect your own. If you find learning to be exciting and worthwhile, he is likely to feel the same way. But he also will mimic your laziness or carelessness. Help him take satisfaction in tasks well done, so that he will want to try more and harder activities. In this way, he will build self-confidence, which, in turn, will give him stability and self-control, the foundation for good discipline.

As he finds that he is in control of what he learns, he will see that sound learning is for his own good. Then, when he is ready for school, he will not be handicapped by the feeling that he is there only because his parents and teachers want him there. He wants to be there himself, and with your encouragement, his zest for learning will not diminish even when he finds some things hard to do. Rather, they will challenge him.

Your child's language and thought processes are now developing in large measure. He has already learned to name many things, including some parts of his body. He can tell you what certain animals say. He has begun to understand and use action words and descriptive words properly; he is learning to speak in sentences. Don't worry about "teaching" him language arts. Simply be conscious of these needs in your conversation with him. If you are friendly and casual and do not criticize him too much, you can get him to talk more freely than if you are overly anxious or formal. He even will repeat sentences after you if you make it a game rather than a lesson. Be careful not to overwhelm him with chatter and complicated sentences. He needs simple, correct sentences, spoken clearly.

Many parents become careless in their day-to-day use of English. They substitute slang or sometimes profanity or they don't bother to use proper language. This can be a serious handicap later to a child, for the child who learns to speak correctly has a great advantage over the child who learns from careless parents.

To familiarize your child with descriptive words, often mention colors of things: "Uncle Tom's car is red"; "this pencil is blue." Use descriptive words throughout the day, and encourage your child to use them. This is the time to help him understand contrasts. Show him a container that is full, and then show it empty. Help him to know what is hard and soft, hot and cold, quiet and loud, new and old, big and little.

Since his infancy, you have been verbalizing your actions—speaking as you act. Now he is ready to use action words also. Continue to talk about what he is doing or what you or others are doing: "I am baking oatmeal cookies"; "you are eating carrot sticks"; "Daddy went to work." Also use words that describe these actions: "Daddy runs fast"; "the kite flies high"; "you came quickly." Ask him to tell what you or others are doing.

When story time comes, have him tell you about the actions he sees in his picture book. You can also cut pictures from magazines showing actions he understands; he can learn to tell you about them in answer to your questions. Here is where 20 or 30 minutes with the parent will do more good for the child than several hours in a preschool.

You can teach him to follow simple directions by having him do errands for you. He probably already understands the simple prepositions such as *in, on, under, over* and *between.* If not, give him practice in both placing and retrieving things, using these words as he acts them out.

Another language hurdle is learning how to make negative statements, such as "The sun is *not* shining," or "The door is *not* open." He will also need practice in forming plurals. You may need to emphasize the final *s* by hissing if the plural has an *s* sound and by buzzing "like a bee" if it has a *z* sound. Then he must learn to use pronouns and verb tenses correctly. He should not, for example, be allowed to say, "Daddy come home" if Daddy has already come. Nor should he say, "He *don't* know" instead of "he *doesn't* know."

In any case, try never to criticize him, interrupt him or correct him while he is talking. You can use his incorrect word correctly in your own sentence, however, without applying it to him. For instance, if he says, "Me like applesauce," you can say, "Yes, I like applesauce, too." Or if he says, "I rided my tricycle fast," you can say, "Yes, you rode it very fast."

If your child has difficulty with a specific sound, make a note of it and, at another time, play a game to help him make that sound. Suppose he says, "witto," instead of "little." He may need tongue exercises. At music time or nap time—when you can sing with him—have him sing a familiar tune, saying "la-la-la" instead of the words, showing him how to open his mouth and put his tongue behind his upper teeth to get a good *l* sound. Also try "loo-loo-loo." But don't try words until you have practiced this on several different occasions. Then have him say words such as "lily," "look," "letter" "little."

Almost all beginning consonants have a sound that is used by animals, or the wind or in some other natural way. You can use those sounds from nature as a basis for practice when there is some difficulty with a certain sound. Geese (and also teakettles) say, "s-s-s-s," dogs pant with an "h-h-h-h" sound, doves say "coo-coo" and so on.

The child, however, should not be made self-conscious about his speech habits. Besides, many of them will disappear if you simply provide a good example. If your child does have a speech or language problem that you cannot handle, seek professional help. Either your physician or your local school superintendent usually can refer you to a qualified person.

One of the great advantages of working together with your child is that learning becomes a natural part of his life. In your close association in your household tasks, if you respond patiently and constructively to your child, you convey attitudes and you teach language as well as facts. Close conversations are now needed more and more to thresh out problems or sooth frustrations. With these measures, you are laying groundwork of companionship that will be especially valuable during the teen-age years.

By the time your helper is 4, he can assume some responsibility as he works with you. It is important that you help him develop this character trait. There are many jobs around the house that are appropriate for his age and ability. He should be made to feel that he is a real part of the family and that his help is needed and appreciated. You should encourage him to work with you, teaching him to use his mind to plan the best way to do his job quickly and well.

He can keep his room, his corner or his own toy box in order. He can become very efficient putting away groceries. He can learn to put away articles such as books, magazines and papers. He can empty trash and garbage and water both indoor and outdoor plants. He can be taught to know the correct place for everything and to help keep everything in its place. Parents have a great opportunity to show the child how work can be fun.

Do not expect your child at this age to do much independent work. He likes and needs to work with you. Such jobs as raking leaves or weeding the garden are too long and tedious for him to do alone. Even though the process may seem simple and easy for you, it becomes a depressing experience for him if you are not there.

He can, however, gradually follow more complicated directions, and you can give him this practice. For instance, "Please get me the hat on my bed." And later, "Please find me the red book on the bottom shelf of my nightstand," or, "The catalogue is under the newspapers in the pantry." Keep your directions difficult enough to be challenging, but not so difficult as to be discouraging. Give your instructions clearly, and train his attention so that you do not have to repeat. If he has trouble remembering, get him to look at you as you tell him. Or perhaps, you are asking too much. In some cases, it may be wise to have him repeat what you have told him. Listening and paying attention are important qualities to develop, for they are basic to success in schoolwork and in life.

The kitchen remains a particularly good place for your child to learn. Here he can distinguish colors, smells, tastes, textures and numbers in a practical way as he helps you cook and learns to do simple cooking procedures himself.

He can also begin to learn some of the simplest facts about food values and how to choose a balanced diet. For instance, he should know that his body is made of the food he eats, and that his bones, teeth, muscles and blood will be only as good as the material he puts into them.

If you are patient and willing to delegate to him the part he is able to do, your child can help you prepare the meals. He can measure such things as flour, sugar, water or milk in various-sized measuring cups or spoons. When fresh vegetables are available, he can help you wash and break green beans into bite-sized pieces for cooking. He can help you scrub carrots with a stiff brush or pad. He can husk corn, wash radishes and shell peas or lima beans. Under your watchful eye, he can do a large share of baking bread, rolls or cookies before he is 5. He can learn to make jello with bananas or to cook oatmeal with raisins. And he can scrub and bake potatoes.

When he sets the table properly, he learns right from left, as well as how to count out the silverware for however many members there are in the family. If you have a guest or two, he is confronted with a problem in adding that is fun to solve. When family members are absent from a meal, he practices subtraction. This way he learns simple solutions to simple problems in natural ways.

If he has been allowed to put away groceries, he can usually find anything you need from the cupboard or refrigerator. As you ask for two apples or three potatoes, he learns the meaning of numbers.

What he can do by himself will depend on how well you have trained him to be careful, neat, thorough—and to clean up afterward. Many 4-year-olds can prepare a simple breakfast of fruit, dry cereal, milk and toast, and can set the table properly and clean up afterward. Most sandwiches are easy for a child to make if he has sliced or prepared fillings to use.

You naturally will have to plan on some spillage and breakage. You will have to be cautious about his using the stove, sharp knives and very hot water. Depending on his maturity, he may have to wait a couple of years before he can use these things. He might be able to use certain electrical appliances before he can safely use the kitchen range. We know a 4-year-old boy who uses an electric blender regularly, measuring several powdered and liquid ingredients for a special family drink. It all depends on the nature and ability of your child, as well as on how you have trained him.

As early as possible, the child should be exposed to the quiet excitement of watching things grow, one of the richest and most fascinating of all childhood experiences. Outdoor garden space is the most ideal, but a few pots or a planter box in the window is sufficient.

If you think you are not enough of a gardener, get advice from someone who is. Try the local librarian or biology teacher, or ask your congressman for government publications. Visit a greenhouse, nursery or a garden or farm. Ask questions. And encourage your child to ask, also. Let your child help when you buy seeds, fertilizer and other supplies. Keep him near you as you read and follow the directions printed on packages of seeds, or as you set out seedlings.

As a beginning, we suggest a minimum of three varieties of seeds, so that your child can see that seeds are different in size and shape, take different amounts of time to grow and produce plants that vary from one another in appearance. For example, radish seeds are of moderate size for vegetables. They germinate in about ten days and are ready to eat in about 25 days. Green bean (Tendergreen) seeds are large, germinate in seven to ten days, and are ready to eat in about 60 days. Also, the Tendergreen variety are bush beans and do not need stakes to support them. You can show how these plants produce their own seeds if you leave a few beans on the plants to mature fully. These mature beans can be dried and planted the following year. Small bulbs, such as onion sets or flower bulbs, are an entirely different kind of "seed."

There are many lessons to be learned from garden projects. Some are profound—that a tiny seed can produce a living plant. On a simpler level, it is a thrill for the young child to see the tiny plants break through the ground. And the excitement continues day after day until he harvests his crop.

You can show your young learner the life-giving power of the sun by putting one plant in a dark room and another in a sunny window. You will enjoy his anticipation from day to day as he watches the differences in color and growth. Have him notice how the leaves turn to the sun. Show him that if he wants a nicely balanced plant indoors, he must turn the plant a quarter turn each day; otherwise, all the leaves will be turning to the sun, and the side next to the sun will grow better than the other side.

You can use the same experiment to show how plants cannot usually grow without water. This can help him learn that he also needs plenty of water and sunshine to be healthy, just as the plants do.

Observing differences in the size, shape and color of plants helps your child learn to discriminate. He will understand better differences in objects, words and letters when it is time for him to learn to read.

Gardening teaches your child some concepts of measurement. Bush beans must be planted two inches deep, three or four inches apart, in rows two feet apart. Radishes need to be planted one-half inch deep, in rows that are one foot apart. When the plants are two inches high, they must be thinned to two inches apart. Your child may not, at first, learn to measure in feet and inches, but he will get the general idea as you use a ruler or a stick of the right length to show him how you do it.

Gardening also helps your child develop patience. Sometimes, he may want to dig up the seed to see what is happening. But he must learn to wait—first for the sprouts to appear, and then for the food to be ready to eat or the flowers to bloom.

He also learns about time relationships—it takes longer for some things to be ready to pick than others. He finds he must be responsible and dependable, for plants must be watered, cultivated and weeded regularly or they may become stunted or die. And he also gains an understanding of where food comes from. When he sees food in the market and helps you prepare it, he knows that someone has had to work to produce it.

When your child is mature enough to help in the care of pets, he is old enough to have one or more of his own. If it is not possible for him to have a dog or a cat, then the care of a bird, a turtle or a couple of fish will delight him and help him develop responsibility and dependability. Or it may be possible for him to share in the care of a neighbor's pets.

Music and musical activities continue to be a valuable means of education, and they should fill a large place in the life of the young child. Develop an enthusiasm for music if possible. At this age, his musical tastes will readily adjust to what he hears in your home. He will enjoy singing alone and with the family. Learn a variety of appropriate songs to teach him.

If you have a musical instrument or record player, he

will enjoy keeping time to the music with blocks to clap together, a drum made out of an oatmeal box, or small pebbles or beans in a container to shake. And remember to have him help you make these instruments. He will also enjoy motion songs and marching to music. But avoid music that is loud or has a heavy, complex beat. It may damage his ears and fray his nerves.

Your child's capacity for stories at this age is almost limitless; he never seems to get enough. And if he is given his choice, you will find that he wants some stories over and over again. The stories he hears have a strong impact on him. So it is wise to continue to choose true stories that teach honesty, dependability, industry and a concern for others. Even true stories should be screened for violence at this age. Nature stories, especially about animals, are among the best for him now. Stories need not always be read from a book, or told while sitting down. While you are sewing, cooking or combing your hair, you can tell your child stories. They may be recollections about himself—which will delight him—or accounts from your own childhood.

Trips are a growing source of pleasure to the child of this age. Your child is old enough now to enjoy family outings to the beach, park, a friend's home or the zoo. Trips with you to the library, the airport, police and fire stations and stores are all pleasant learning experiences that do not involve any pressure to learn. But he should be expected to control himself. For example, he should not touch or beg for things at the store. And he must obey promptly for safety's sake. It will be easier for you if you make it consistently clear that well-behaved children are allowed to go places more often. Such trips help him build a rich background for language development. They also supplement the ideas and facts he learns from stories and from the conversation of adults. You can strengthen the impact of these experiences by talking about them after you arrive home or reviewing them the next day.

Everyday activities provide you with the opportunity to establish some early numbers concepts that will be invaluable to your child when it is time for formal arithmetic. In addition to the learning situations already mentioned in the sections on gardening and kitchen work, there are many other chances to use numbers, measurements and comparisons of distance, size and weight. (Comparisons of all kinds can be taught effectively at this age. Usually by the time a child is 5, he should understand the meanings of big-little, short-tall, heavy-light, empty-full, far-near and large-small.)

At mealtime, help him count the crackers or cookies that you give him. Divide an apple or other piece of food into halves and quarters with a casual remark, "You have half, and I will have half." Or "There are four of us for lunch, so we will cut this in four pieces. We can each have one-fourth."

He will have fun counting blocks to see how many he can stack before they fall down. He should be able to tell his age and hold up the corresponding number of fingers. You can also help him count his fingers and toes. Sing counting songs like "Five Little Chickadees," or "Ten Little Indians." Since all children like to keep track of their growth, you can record your child's progress by making marks on a closet doorpost or on a wall. He gets the idea of measure and weight when he hears you say he has grown an inch or gained a pound. He also will be fascinated if you measure yourself or another member of the family.

A small child needs to be prepared for special events. While he loves surprises in the form of little presents, special treats or simple home activities, he seldom reacts well to the surprise of having company, going to the dentist or doctor or embarking on a trip. He will do much better if he is told what is going to happen and what you expect of him.

Anticipation is often a greater treat than the actual happening. The child likes to talk and to hear you talk about the things you will be doing. Perhaps you will want your child to get ready for bed before company comes, then greet the guests when they arrive, and soon go to bed. If he knows this ahead of time and recognizes that this is expected of him, he will usually cooperate nicely. If he has no previous warning, you seldom will have an easy time.

When you take your child with you on a visit, he should be told as much about the place as he is able to understand. If there are no children at your destination, he should take with him a few small toys—if he can help select these toys, all the better. Even if there are children, it still may be wise to have him take a toy or two. He should be given some idea ahead of time of what he should do when he gets there, and how you expect him to behave.

Foresight is one of the parents' finest tools. If you provide your child with the proper environment and discipline at home, he will seldom embarrass or disappoint you away from home. Your child wants your approval and will strive to deserve it if you encourage him by your smiles and words. And he will actually learn self-respect as he learns to respect you.

14.

Age 4 to Age 7

When your child reaches age 5 or 6, he seems quite mature and sure of himself. He can take care of most of his personal needs—washing, dressing and toileting. He is generally dependable. And he is so bright! Compared with the toddler he was only recently, you may be tempted to assume that he should be put into school. You will also feel social pressure from some of your friends who will insist that he should be sent to kindergarten to fulfill his curiosity and zest for learning, or to help him socially.

Yet the separation from home, the overstimulation of the group, the pressure of competition for the teacher's attention and for the equipment, and the close eye-work is not normally good for the child at this age. Early schooling can, and often does, slow the momentum of his intellectual growth and creativity. There is reason to believe that the thrill the youngster finds in experimenting with the natural things about him at home is soon stifled by the distractions and regimentation of the typical school program.

A wholesome home, on the other hand, can provide stability so that, in a few more years, he will be better able to cope with school! Some will say you are being overprotective. Not so. You are simply decreasing the child's chances of being hurt, until he is ready at age 8 or later for the complex experience that is school.

At ages 4 to 7, a child's heart grows relatively rapidly, although, in general, the body is growing much more slowly than before. The most noticeable change is that your child begins to lose his babylike contours, as his trunk, arms and legs lengthen. His baby teeth are also being replaced by his permanent ones. The quality of these second teeth will depend largely on his early nutrition.

His eyes are not yet ready for much near work. He actually has a tendency to be far-sighted, for his eyes are relatively shallow in depth, not yet mature in either size or shape, and the eyeballs and eye lenses are still quite plastic. Near-sightedness may develop if he does much close work, watches television a great deal or stays inside where he cannot habitually focus at some distance.

Although his eye-hand coordination is steadily improving, he is not yet ready for systematic writing. His large muscles still are better developed than his small ones, although by the time he is about 8 his small muscles will be much improved. About the age of 4 or 5, he clearly shows a preference for his left or his right hand. Normally, you should make no effort to change this.

The child is very active and cannot be expected to stay still or maintain attention for long periods. The capacity for longer periods of quiet and attention is increasing, however.

For the typical child, physical development remains uneven throughout this 4-to-7 age, which partly accounts for the fact that he is especially susceptible to respiratory diseases. This is another reason to keep him home: You give him more time to build immunities and his strength before he is exposed to diseases and other physical hazards at school.

Irregular growth rate still appears evident, not only in the physical development of your child, but also in his mental, emotional and social development. Because he seems mature for his age in one respect does not mean that he is mature in others. Even children within a family mature differently, developing such skills as walking and talking, at different rates. It is important to understand this and to deal with each child accordingly.

This range in development is another reason why many young children cannot cope successfully with school. Entirely too often a child has gone to school with enthusiasm and been sadly disillusioned by failure in the first grade. Boys are in the majority of those suffering in the first grade, largely because boys at this age are six to twelve-months less mature than girls. Many first-grade teachers and the materials they use are geared to the average 6½-year-old-girl; yet, more often than not, both boys and girls are exposed to the same reading program. Even if the wise teacher knows better than to try to teach reading to all first-graders, she is under pressure from parents, school board members and the children themselves—all of whom have been conditioned to the "necessity" of learning skills in the first grade.

REACTIONS THAT MAY BE EXPECTED

At this age, your child has enormous curiosity and initiative. He also has a lot of energy and is not able to sit and listen for very long. In his activities, he is likely to be more interested in the process than in the outcome. For instance, he often likes kneading and shaping the bread dough even more than seeing the finished buns. Yet, increasingly, he will learn to find satisfaction in the conclusion of his project, especially if other members of the family compliment him on the good buns he helped to make and ask him how *he* likes them.

He continues to grow more independent and can take more responsibility. However, he often forgets and, therefore, needs adult supervision. Patient guidance can make his work more efficient and purposeful. Now and for several years to come, he will work best with you, for your companionship is an important part of his development. Also because of his short periods of interest, he cannot usually complete an activity by himself. Your help and encouragement are vital in helping him establish the habit of following through.

Children of both sexes still play well together, but there are increasing differences in their interests and activities. Our culture has encouraged girls to play with dolls and "girl toys," and boys to imitate cowboys, firemen, or Indians and prefer "boy toys," with obvious results. In any event, boys are more conscious than girls about the differences in toys. Even when they play together, boys will be likely to assume male roles when playing store or house, and will play more actively and roughly than girls.

Your child's sense of time is now maturing. He also is able to understand something about the use of money. He can see the need for safety and will, with your guidance, take reasonable precautions. Because he is often preoccupied and forgetful, however, he still needs your watchfulness and reminders.

He now particularly wants and needs your approval. He is concerned about right and wrong and is developing a conscience, the quality of which is dependent, to a large degree, on the quality and the consistency of your example.

If you send him to school during this period, you will find that he will move from dependence on your approval to dependence on the approval of the children at school. He will become more subject to their influences and pressures. At this age, before he has firmly established his own moral code, these outside influences can be negative. He needs a relatively uninterrupted period to gradually learn respect, obedience and self-control. Your steady hand, without unnecessary influence from others, will help him develop all-around stability. He can better establish sound values, and grow in balance mentally and physically.

If you have been reasonably consistent, he has developed some sense of fairness and some understanding of the value of rules. He even likes to make rules, and he should be allowed to help you make them. He is now capable of constructive self-criticism. He is beginning to reason systematically, although he will not be fully reasonable until he is 8 years old or older. He may not be genuinely responsible until 10 or 11. In dealing with him you should, however, make use of his emerging ability to reason. If you have taught him the basics of self-control, you will probably find him genuinely cooperative at this age. Discipline will not be a major problem.

NEEDS OF THIS AGE

Since physical maturity varies in different children and cannot be forced, the best way you can help your child is to provide him with many opportunities for activity. He needs to develop his large muscles by making and doing things with his hands. Since his muscles are not completely developed, he will probably be awkward and clumsy. Don't pressure him beyond his ability or expect much skill or control. He needs to experience success in his projects.

He continues to thrive under a regular home routine, where he knows what to expect and has the security of wise and loving parents. He needs fair, gentle, but firm and consistent discipline. Harshness, impatience, inconsistency, or severity will discourage and dishearten him. Keep your rules few and well-made. Because he is eager to learn and has many interests, you should take advantage of his enthusiasm to build up his background of experience and knowledge. This should be done without pressure or domination, letting his natural curiosity lead the way. He will learn most by doing what he enjoys most, and he will enjoy most what he is able to do best.

Be sure you still accept him at his own level of accomplishment and give him the encouragement he needs to finish the tasks or projects he starts. He should not be urged to attempt tasks beyond his ability; but when he is frustrated by something he is doing, he should be helped to try to overcome the problem by looking for another solution or by getting assistance, rather than by giving up, losing his temper or daydreaming. His satisfaction in seeing a project completed will stimulate him to greater effort next time.

Competition or group pressures to do what he is not yet capable of doing often cause him to become tense and to lose confidence in himself, which may have far-reaching, damaging results. More than ever, he needs success experiences. He also needs to be given certain responsibilities within his ability, without unnecessary interference or too many directions, restrictions or criticisms. As with all of us, he is likely to resent being told over and over again what he already knows or is already planning to do.

Your good example is the best way to teach him the manners and habits that you want him to have, supplemented by voiced approval of his good qualities, and gentle reminders when necessary.

As the child begins to reason consistently, he should be helped to understand *why* certain things are required. He will then begin to use his developing powers to make decisions about acceptable behavior, which, in turn, will help him to accept orders and to carry them out without argument. It is well to offer the "whys" first without waiting for him to demand them.

During these years, your family system of government should gradually change from a benevolent dictatorship to a true democracy where your child learns to understand the rights of each member of the family and to give and take. Such an atmosphere requires learning to work out solutions to problems, taking into consideration the rights of both parent and child. You will find that with problems that arise suddenly, thoughtful questions in place of a snap judgment often will enable you to avoid a conflict. As your child grows older, he will become even more cooperative if he is allowed to communicate. This is especially true if you are reasonable in finding a compromise or substitute for an unacceptable situation.

It usually is best to let children resolve their own arguments between themselves. In case it is necessary to intervene, it is wise not to set yourself up as a judge or decision-maker. Listen carefully, help them to communicate and come to their own decisions, incidentally teaching them consideration for others.

Your child still needs 11 to 12 hours of sleep each day, and part of this is best gained by a midday nap. While this may not be the practice in your neighborhood, such rest means much to the building of a strong body and mind.

PLAYTHINGS

Your child now has the physical skills to use a bicycle, roller skates, ice skates, sled, balls of different types, a jump rope and even a baseball bat. What will be practical and safe for him will depend on your particular living area.

He will continue to enjoy the usual playground equipment, and the boxes, ladder and other home equipment described in the previous chapter. He will enjoy building with Lincoln Logs, Tinker Toys, or Erector Sets. You will need access to more books, which you can read to him in answer to his many questions. Take time to get acquainted with the local library.

Because he can now assume a reasonable amount of responsibility in caring for pets, he will benefit from having one of his own. An animal such as a cat or dog that can respond actively to his love and attention is preferable. If this is impractical, even a fish, a bird, gerbils, a hamster or a turtle make excellent little friends who will be dependent on him. Pets help him to feel needed, and caring for them helps him develop a sense of responsibility.

Help him to follow his natural interests in wildlife. Even in a city apartment, you may be able to lure birds and even a squirrel to a feeder attached to the outside of your window. The feeder can be made by cutting an empty gallon milk carton or plastic jug. If you have a place for one, a birdbath provides a good opportunity for pleasurable learning, especially if you have a pair of binoculars to give you a close-up view.

Your child is undoubtedly interested in collecting things—shells, leaves, seeds, rocks, wildflowers. He can use some of these things in his art work. You should provide a place for him to keep his collections in an orderly way, even if it is under his bed. Collecting is one of his natural interests that you can use to build his store of information. Illustrated books can help him identify his specimens. He will learn to compare and recognize similarities and differences in shape, size and general appearance. Later, this visual training will help him in discriminating between letters of the alphabet and words.

ACTIVITIES AND OPPORTUNITIES

Play is important, but at this age so is useful work, which provides one of the most effective opportunities to establish habits of dependability, neatness, promptness, thoroughness, and industry. It is true that it will take some planning to devise means to keep your child usefully busy. Let him know that he is a partner in the family firm. Show your appreciation for little things well done—and watch his delight. Show him how to do his work in the most efficient way, rather than in a careless manner. He wants and needs your approval. The fact that other children may not have similar responsibilities should not be allowed to discourage him. Help him to understand that work is a privilege, that it makes him a better person.

But don't assign him tasks and then walk away to let him work alone. One of the greatest advantages of family teamwork is the opportunity for a friendly relationship with your children. This is an investment that will pay off in the years ahead.

Take time to play daily with your youngsters, but realize that it is seldom possible to sit down and have a confidential chat at playtime. While you work together, however, there is time for close conversation and building of mutual confidence. The generation gap is bridged more often over the kitchen sink than on the baseball diamond.

Your child can become involved in everything you

normally do in the way of work at home, including gardening, sewing and woodwork. He can learn by example how to become "Mr. Fixit" around the house. You may not be skilled in any of these activities, but the knowledge you have or can easily get is enough to satisfy your child for some time. Although, as we have noted, it is unwise to teach your child to read at an early age, his ultimate success in reading will depend largely on his background of experiences and his language development. He needs to see, feel, smell, touch and taste things in the world around him and to acquire the language skill to communicate well orally before he will be ready to attempt the complex task of reading for himself.

You have been giving him training in listening carefully, and he has learned to follow directions. He may even have learned to follow a simple recipe in the kitchen. Now he should also have opportunities to *give* directions—in how to do things and how to get to familiar places such as the store, post office or church. Give him practice in carrying simple oral messages to another member of the family or to a neighbor.

You are an important teacher at this age, and there are constant opportunities for great teaching, if you are alert. For example, give him opportunities to express himself without interruption or correction when he has something to tell. If he gets mixed up in the sequence of events, gently ask him questions to help him organize his "report."

When he has things he would like to tell friends or relatives who live far away, let him dictate a letter for you to write. Perhaps he can draw a picture to enclose. Then let him stamp the envelope and mail it.

If he wants to learn how to write his name, teach him, using large manuscript (printing) letters written with a large pencil or crayon on a big sheet of paper. If he asks what certain words on labels or signs say, tell him. Whatever he asks about and wishes to learn, teach him in a casual, matter-of-fact way, but do not push him beyond his capacity. He may teach himself to read. Yet he should not be allowed more than fifteen or 20 minutes at a time with books if eyestrain is to be avoided at this age.

When story hour comes, give him opportunities to discuss or repeat portions of the story and to answer questions. He sometimes should have practice in retelling a story he has heard or recounting a recent experience he has had. He might do this the next day, while you and he are working in the garden or the kitchen. Such a report tests his recall and his ability to tell the events in the proper order. Ask him why certain characters acted as they did. Ask other questions to stimulate thinking, especially questions that ask "why?" Acting out certain appropriate stories with you or other members of the family is another worthwhile activity.

If he has not already learned to handle the telephone, he should be taught to answer politely and correctly, such as, "This is the Jones' place, Johnny speaking." And when someone else is asked for, he answers, "Just a minute, please." If the person is not there, he answers, "He isn't here right now. Would you like to talk to my mother?" or "Would you like to leave a message?" Have pretend conversations with him to give him practice, and occasionally, phone him from another place for practice. Compliment him on what he has done well, and carefully correct him where needed. This is a quality of teaching that few preschools can provide as well as you.

He should also know how or where to call in case of emergency. He should learn your first and last names. He should also know his own phone number and his address. This will involve recognizing and perhaps learning to write the numbers, but this should come in his own good time, as he needs and wants to know them, without pressure from you.

During these years, he becomes old enough to learn how to be a good host. Let him introduce a child to you or a child to another child, and acknowledge introductions of himself. He should be helped to pronounce names clearly and should be encouraged to smile, shake hands correctly and be friendly. Your good example and preparation beforehand are the keys to success. Our visitors used to be charmed by our 4-year-old when she led them by the hand to the sofa. After they were seated, she crawled up beside them with a book to entertain them. Of course, there must be limits. Our child was seldom allowed to be the center of activity.

Conversations at the family mealtime can be influential in the language development of a child as well as in the development of his attitudes and outlook. Try to have the family together at mealtime at least once a day, and enlist the cooperation of the older members to keep the atmosphere calm, unhurried and pleasant. Guide the conversation along constructive lines, respecting each one's right to speak.

You can have fun helping the child develop his memory by teaching him simple poems or verses. First say the whole verse to him so that he can get the meaning. Then have him repeat *short* but complete phrases after you, one or two times each day. After several days, he will be able to say the whole verse alone. Let him repeat these poems often to you and to other family members, as a review and also to give him a feeling of success.

Since the stories heard and the verses learned at this age are usually remembered for life, it is important that they be constructive rather than silly. Children can learn meaningful verses from such inspirational books as the Bible, the Torah, or the Koran as easily and happily as they can talk.

There are many games you can play that will teach your child to listen. They can be played while you are washing the dishes, bathing a younger sibling, or riding in a bus. One such game might be, "Let's see how many things we can think of (or see) that begin like 'bunny.'" Or each person can name several things that begin like his own name. These activities train the ear to discriminate between sounds and are a very important preparation for later reading.

Another valuable ear-training activity is to give your child chances to hear and appreciate rhyme and rhythm. He can learn to identify the rhyming words in poems that you read to him. Or he might enjoy supplying the missing word in a made-up rhyme: "I need a light to read at_____(night)"; "It's much too far without a_____ (car")"; or "Please be quick to bring me a_____(stick)."

A variation of this game is to say, "I see something that rhymes with_____," or "I'm thinking of an animal whose name rhymes with_____." Sometimes, you can just see how many words you both can think of that rhyme with "cat," "bill," "play," and so on. Have him mark the score on a piece of paper.

You can teach manners and other bits of wisdom with rhymes. Some parents, for example, care that their children learn to eat their soup by moving the spoon away from them instead of toward them. This can be taught with a simple rhyme: "Like little boats push out to sea, I push my spoon away from me." And bedtime sometimes comes easier with, "Early to bed and early to rise, makes a child healthy, happy and wise" (apologies to Benjamin Franklin).

Similar games can also give your child an opportunity to hear and identify various sounds. One of you can make a sound and have the other one imitate and identify it— telling what animal, insect, bird or object makes the sound. He can learn to recognize sounds of vehicles;

sounds of musical instruments; sounds of the weather (wind, rain, hail, thunder); and sounds of water (trickling brook, leaking faucet, rushing waterfall, ocean waves); sounds of people (whisper, shout, cry, cough, sneeze, moan); sounds of work (sawing, pounding, drilling, sanding) and ordinary household sounds (broom sweeping, toaster popping up, air conditioner, electric mixer, alarm clock, electric fan).

Talk about the sounds and let your child explain what they tell us. He should be able to describe them as being soft or loud, high or low, short or long, and sometimes, to use other more colorful descriptive words. Our son used to make up some of his own words, such as "Wasn't that a funny *snocker* noise?"

The child's eyes, as well as his ears, can be trained at this age. Even though he should not do much near work or be confined indoors for long periods of time, remember that he is curious, and that there are many opportunities for visual experiences that do not harm his eyes. He should not only learn to recognize but should be able to name the basic colors and use them in his conversation. He can also recognize similarities and differences in the appearance of things, comparing size and shapes. He can learn to identify birds, trees (by their shapes, their bark, their fruit and their leaves), flowers, shells, rocks, fish, insects or animals as he pursues his natural inclination for collecting. If he is given pictures of things, try to find reasonably large, colorful ones to avoid eye strain.

When bad weather keeps him indoors, he will enjoy making scrapbooks out of old magazines. He can learn how to organize things by having one book or section for flowers, one for animals (perhaps divided by zoo, farm and pet animals) and one for birds. A clothing book can be divided into winter and summer clothes, furniture into that found in different rooms of the house. A food scrapbook can be organized into the four food groups of a balanced diet—milk and cheese, protein foods, breads and cereals, fruits and vegetables. This can be a means of learning simple nutritional principles. Another book could be about himself, with photographs and pictures he draws of his experiences. Let him dictate captions for you to print.

Another exercise in discrimination and organization is sorting buttons, nails, screws, bolts and nuts. Or your child might like to arrange canned goods in different sections or rows, according to their category. He may not yet be able to read words, but he can see patterns.

The senses of taste, smell and touch seldom can be as thoroughly developed in the schoolroom as at home. Your child should be able to identify most familiar foods by taste alone. It is easy to check whether he can by playing little games with him. When it is mealtime, have him shut his eyes or temporarily wear a blindfold while you give him a taste of what he is going to be eating to see if he can identify it. He should be able to describe food as crisp or crunchy, soft or hard, hot or cold, wet or dry, sweet or sour.

Many foods and other household items can be identified by smell—perfume, soap, baby powder, rubbing alcohol, vinegar, onions, burned toast, bread or cake baking, peanuts, popcorn. Stimulate your child's awareness by such questions as "What do you think is in the oven?" or "Can you smell what is cooking?"

He can develop his sense of touch by learning to put a few large bolts and nuts together while blindfolded—an activity that also gives him practice using his small muscles. Without the blindfold, he can learn to decide by looking which nut fits on which bolt.

In school many children are confused and frustrated by their efforts to add and subtract numerals in the first grade. Numerals are merely symbols of amounts, and try-ing to understand the relationship of these symbols to actual experience is probably a strain for a 6-year-old. He is forced to work with theoretical problems that are not yet easy for him to perceive. As a result of his premature efforts, he may hate math for the rest of his life. Whereas, at home, he can be given plenty of opportunity for count-ing, dividing and measuring in his work and play, so that recognizing and writing numerals will have practical meaning to him as he needs and wants to use those skills.

As it becomes convenient and helpful, teach your child about time. You can use a clock with large numbers, or you and he can make a paper-plate clock with large numbers and movable hands. You might start with, "When the little hand gets to three and the big hand points straight up, it will be three o'clock and then we will go." Or, "When both hands are pointing straight up, it will be lunchtime—twelve o'clock." As his need and his inter-est develop, he can learn about half-hours and quarter-hours, and can learn to count by fives and even by min-utes. Many radio stations announce the exact time at frequent intervals, and you can let him listen to a radio "time check" to determine whether your clock is slow or fast.

You can acquaint your child with the days of the week by mentioning the name of each day in the morn-ing. Normally, there will be certain days that have special significance because of regular activities on that day—perhaps you all go to church or to the library. Give him a calendar of his own, preferably one with large numbers and letters, so he can mark off each day and change the page at the end of the month.

This may be the period for your child to learn some-thing about money and its use. He may be given a weekly allowance and helped to budget it, dividing it among a charity offering, savings and something he needs or wants to give to others. He should have enough freedom to learn from the experience, but enough guidance to make the experience practical. One caution: extra handouts, when he has spent his money, will not teach him to plan wisely.

One area of elementary science to introduce to the child at this age is the study of weather. His awareness of the weather also can be helpful, particularly if he learns to associate weather with the kind of clothes to wear. Invite him to tell you when to wear a raincoat and take an umbrella. Discuss the weather each day with him. Listen to the radio or TV weather report and forecast. If possible, secure a large indoor-outdoor thermometer for him to watch; perhaps, he can record the temperature over a period of time.

Study about the seasons together. If you live where there is snowfall, catch a few snowflakes on a dark cloth or garment and look at them through a magnifying glass. Notice that some flakes stick together or are broken in falling, but that each perfect flake has six sides. And no two are alike.

Six-sided "snowflakes" can easily be cut out of square white or colored paper, folded first in half and then in three's. Let your child use blunt-end scissors to cut many different snowflake designs. Then use his designs for decoration on the table, on the windows or hanging from thread in a doorway.

Observe the clouds and teach him the story they tell about the weather. On a cool morning, show him how the warm air he breathes out meets the cold air and makes a little cloud. The same thing happens when a teakettle begins to boil. Relate these events to the clouds in the sky. You can learn these and many other interesting things about the weather from books at your library.

Talk about the effect of the seasons on plants, animals

and people. Even if you do not live where the seasons are distinct, there are usually some significant weather changes during the year, with corresponding changes in the habits of animals and birds in your area.

The study of anatomy and physiology, in an informal and practical way, is valuable to your child, not only because it relates to his own health but also because rudimentary knowledge now will help avoid embarrassment and confusion later on. Teach him the names for the parts of his body and the tasks they perform. Help him understand that there are some things we do not discuss outside the family, not because they are "nasty," but because they are "special" or "private." Since he is becoming a reasonable person, he can understand principles of hygiene and sanitation. He can begin to understand why we wash our hands before eating and after toileting, why we do not use the dishcloth to wipe up the floor and why we cover our mouths when coughing and sneezing.

He can also understand the function of blood. He can, learn that at any given moment, a large share of our blood goes to the part of the body where the activity is the greatest. So when our stomach is full, much of the blood goes to the stomach to help digest our food. That is why it is not good to play hard or swim immediately after eating; for then, the blood has to leave the stomach and go to other parts of the body, and the food cannot be properly digested. The result sometimes is a stomach ache or cramps or just an uncomfortable feeling. Your 6-year-old can also understand why we cannot do our best thinking or studying when our stomach is full, because the blood that is needed by the brain when we think is being used elsewhere in the body. That is also a reason why we do not eat between meals.

As your child works or plays, you will probably hear him humming or singing songs he has learned. He will enjoy many kinds of songs, including lullabies, patriotic songs and singing games, but songs should be short, simple and pitched in a medium range. His musical standard will reflect precisely what you provide. Some musicians feel that musical ability is not so much inherited as it is developed. In any case, nearly everyone has the capacity to appreciate good music, and many can find it a valuable method of creative expression.

Give the child opportunities to respond to the rhythms of various types of music by marching, tiptoeing or clapping. When appropriate, show him how to gallop like a horse, fly like a bird, sway like a tree. He will still enjoy simple rhythm instruments made from ordinary household items: a drum from an oatmeal box or coffee can, sticks to strike together, or something to shake made from a plastic or metal container filled with beans or gravel.

As in almost every other type of learning, a child's exposure to music early in life establishes a base on which to build greater enjoyment and abilities all through his life. Teach him the names of the most common musical instruments and help him to identify them by their sounds. However, his eye-hand and ear-hand coordination are not yet well enough established for him to learn to play an instrument well. Even if you feel he has special talents, you will save time, money and nervous energy (your own and his), and possibly prevent failure, if you delay formal music lessons until he is between 8 and 11 years old; and usually, the later the better.

By this time, your child has a reasonable understanding of the dependence of family members on one other, and he recognizes his place and his responsibilities in the family. Now he needs to learn about various people in the community and to appreciate the services they provide. This can best be taught by short trips to the fire station, post office, police station, hospital or farm, with conversations, if possible, with the workers, and discussions at home afterward.

If he has not already had the opportunity to help others outside the family, he should be given the chance to do kind things for others, especially for those who are old, sick, poor or otherwise disadvantaged. He should learn never to ridicule a person who is poor or handicapped. Teach him that if he has vegetables or fruit in his garden, he can share his harvest, that part of his allowance can be spent for a card for someone who is sick, that outgrown clothes can be cleaned and given to someone who can wear them, and that little handmade items can show his concern for someone who is lonely or shut in.

Art can become a means of self-expression, of experimenting and creating, for your child. All you really need to provide is a positive atmosphere, some inexpensive materials such as sand or flour or paper, a place to use or display his creations and a few ideas gleaned from children's books or magazines. Making useful things brings the child special satisfaction. He can make gifts or holiday decorations, or he can draw designs on paper napkins, or make paper-towel place mats to be used for dinner.

The child who is kept constructively busy at work or play is usually a well-behaved youngster. This does not mean that you have to be a hovering parent. He needs time alone, a lot of it. But if you are aware of his needs and share in their fulfillment *without worrying about them,* the chances are that you will be one of those parents who delights in children of this age.

15.

Age 6 to Age 8 or 9

If the groundwork has been carefully and consistently laid, even allowing for parental error, the child, at age 6 to 8 is a pleasant companion and an efficient helper. He is increasingly responsible and dependable. He has learned to do many things for himself and for others, including household chores. He is working toward independence, although he still needs the leadership and guidance of adults. As he is able to accept greater responsibility, he can be given greater freedom. Too much direction or criticism can be damaging to him, but wise nurturing of his enthusiasm and curiosity will bring growth and achievement.

The growth rate in this age group is even slower than previously, possibly only two or three inches in height and three to six pounds in weight per year, with girls continuing to mature more rapidly than boys. By this time the child's lungs and digestive and circulatory systems may be almost mature in their functions. His energy level is high, but because his heart is not yet fully mature, care must be taken not to let him overexert himself or become too tired. He should be taught not to lift objects that are too heavy. Boys especially should be taught to keep their legs together when they lift heavy objects, in order to avoid hernias. Naps are still preferable; at least, he should have a quiet rest time in the middle of the day.

During this period, your child's eyes are still developing in both size and shape. Consequently, too much reading or other near work should be avoided. Also, his eye-hand and small-muscle coordination are still developing. It is not always easy for him to manage precise movements, such as those required by handwriting, without strain. For this reason, delaying formal reading and the usual school work until the child is 8 years old produces better physical and emotional health and guarantees a much greater possibility of later success.

REACTIONS THAT MAY BE EXPECTED

At this age, a child normally has a strong sense of fairness and of right and wrong. You will have to be careful about making promises you cannot keep, threats you do not carry out or any discipline or treatment that is not fair or straightforward. Games you play must follow the rules unless the participants agree ahead of time on a variation.

Because of his great amount of energy and his desire to do gymnastics, climb trees, ride a two-wheel bicycle or jump off high places, he can be expected to have some accidents. His knowledge of safety principles and his use of common sense will bring him through this period. He should understand that it is dangerous to play in some areas. He should be fully aware of such hazards as open wells, dumps, ponds, water tanks and trunks or refrigerators. A true knowledge of what is dangerous produces caution. Lack of knowledge, on the other hand, leads either to fear or recklessness, depending on the child's nature.

He is eager and ambitious, sometimes attempting more than he can handle and then getting discouraged if he cannot do it well. Often, a little help and encouragement at the right time can motivate him to follow through and achieve his goal. He is able to maintain relatively long periods of attention if the project is within his ability and of interest to him.

NEEDS OF THIS AGE

The large muscles are still developing, so the child needs much outdoor activity, both in work and play. Fences and trees to climb and chores to do help him work off his energy and exercise his muscles. So does a neighborhood park or a vacant lot fixed up and supervised by a group of cooperative parents.

It is well to get him interested in the development of his body. The desire to grow up and have a strong body is a powerful incentive for most children to participate in worthwhile activities. Try having him do push-ups, sit-ups and other calisthenics with you each day when the weather is bad or when other opportunities are unavailable. When possible, he should do these exercises near an open window.

If your child gets plenty of rest, has been properly nourished and lives in a reasonably calm environment, he should not develop any posture problems. But he needs to be aware of the importance of standing and sitting correctly for health reasons. It will help him walk and stand correctly if he imagines his body as being suspended by a string from the top of the head. Balancing a book on the head to practice smooth, graceful walking is also helpful.

His ability to reason is developing, and he likes to talk things over. He better recognizes others' needs and rights and is more willing to compromise when he has disagreements. He should be allowed to make choices, although still within limits you set. Give him a choice of two or three things, all of which are acceptable to you. He needs incentives for doing his chores, keeping his room clean and behaving acceptably. The best incentives will be your encouragement and praise, and his own success in the projects and jobs he attempts.

PLAYTHINGS

Additional playthings that are nice but not essential at this age are kites, tops, marbles and possibly a croquet set, if you have a place to use it. There are also table games and easy games of skill that he will enjoy with other members of the family, such as tiddlywinks, Chinese checkers and games that teach numbers and letters. A basketball backboard and basket mounted away from windows takes up only a small amount of space and provides good exercise and training in accuracy.

Children of this age enjoy cutting out paper dolls and playing with a dollhouse, which can be made of wooden crates and furnished with cardboard furniture. They also can become very creative with a box of old clothes for dress-up, and a variety of arts and crafts materials.

Toward the end of this period, your child will want to become more skillful in sports—swimming, skating or ball playing. He needs practice, and perhaps a little coaching and encouragement from you, but no pressure. Striving to reach an appropriate personal standard is a much better incentive for him than competition against another child.

ACTIVITIES AND OPPORTUNITIES

Almost all the activities listed in earlier chapters can be expanded for the child in the beginning of this age group. As before, he learns best by discovery and by doing.

Work still comes at the head of the list. Handled wisely, it is the best experience a young child can have. He is able to be a real help with washing the car or cleaning up the yard, preparing a meal, packing for a trip, or cleaning the house. In fact, he can share in almost everything that needs to be done around the home. In general, you should not do jobs that your child can do for himself or for the family, as long as he is not actually overworked. Most jobs, however, are far more enjoyable if done with you rather than alone.

Girls and boys of this age can learn how to use tools effectively in the home, so that they can make simple repairs when necessary. They can learn how to fix an electric plug, a leaky faucet or a squeaky or sticking door, and how to sew on a button, darn a sock or mend a tear in a garment.

As the child enlarges his activities, safety principles become even more important. He will need to learn the rules for whatever tool or machine he uses, and he will need supervision until he understands clearly what is necessary and is willing to abide by the rules. He must know, for instance, that he should not use electrical appliances near water in the tub or sink. And he should learn how to anticipate the likelihood of danger and avoid it.

Often children in Western countries become aware

of auto-driving principles at this time, and your example will be very effective in establishing his future behavior behind the wheel. Your attitude toward speed limits, cautions and other restrictions, as well as your general consideration of others on the road, will be indelibly impressed on his mind. Most driving signs are now in the form of pictures, and he will like to interpret these as well as read the ones that have words on them. Since he is normally far-sighted at this age, he may be able to see them better than you.

These are the years when children really begin to enjoy camping. Planning the food and packing the gear for a camping trip provide valuable training in organization. Sharing in camp cooking, camp chores and other typical camping experiences draws the family together. Following a hiking trail, using a compass, reading and following a simple map and studying nature are all exciting learning experiences. At a time when we are in danger of losing many of our natural resources, we need also to teach the importance of conserving our wildlife, streams and forests. This is an excellent time for him to learn about the balance of nature and the ways all of us can help to preserve our environment. And leaving a campsite or other public facility cleaner than you found it is a practical way of teaching consideration for others.

This may be the time to introduce some simple information about astronomy. For example, you can easily find, or learn how to locate, the Big and Little Dippers, the Milky Way, Jupiter and the North Star. As your child's interest develops, you can learn more from a child's book on astronomy. If there is an observatory or planetarium nearby, make use of it.

The study of spiders and how they construct their webs is also fascinating to most children. First you must be sure you can identify the few spiders that are poisonous; in every case, be careful. Spiders can be kept alive and comfortable in a fruit jar with holes in the cover for air, water in a piece of damp cotton or sponge and insects for food. Your child can even preserve the spider's delicate work of art. First spray the web until it is sticky with white shellac; then, press a piece of black cardboard against it. The web will stick to the cardboard, after which you can carefully cover the card with transparent contact paper.

Since children like to cook, watch for simple recipes that your child can make, either alone or with a minimum of supervision, so that he feels he has made a real contribution to a meal. The family should let him know that they enjoy his cooking. One 8-year-old we know specializes in lasagna; another younger child tears lettuce and adds cherry tomatoes and ready-made croutons for a tossed salad and another likes to make a favorite family roast.

Give a child practice waiting on the family at mealtime. He will gain skill and self-confidence. With a little briefing beforehand, you might find that he makes an excellent assistant at the table when you have company for dinner. He can help set the table and pour the beverage; he can keep the glasses refilled, clear off the table before the dessert and serve the dessert. You will be proud of his performance as you relax and enjoy your guests. He will be happy in the satisfaction of a job well done.

This is considered the golden age for memory. Now your child can probably memorize more quickly and remember longer than at any other time in his life. Not only that, he enjoys memorizing such things as the scout pledge and motto, the Pledge of Allegiance, and children's poems.

During this period, your child can learn much more about the value of money. He can learn true economy in a practical way by setting aside part of his money for certain necessary purposes, part for helping others, and part for himself. Parents can help him learn to spend his money wisely and to keep accounts of his income and his spending.

As he has grown older, his horizons have gradually broadened so that now he is interested in people farther away from home and even in other parts of the world. Books, pictures and personal experiences will help him understand and appreciate people of other cultures, and will add interest to his study of geography. Some families deliberately seek out people of other nationalities. You might invite a family from another country to your home; you might even ask your guests to wear their native costumes and bring some handicraft or typical item from their country. Your guests might well return the invitation, so that you, in turn, can see and hear more about their country.

Pride in, and loyalty to, his country are easily developed in a child of this age. He should carefully be taught respect for his country and its flag. Acquaint him with simple stories about the beginnings of his country and the making of the flag. Teach him what liberty means in terms of both rules and rights. Help him to understand that he is not free unless he defends the freedom of others—at home, at school, on the highway or wherever he goes. Celebrate patriotic occasions by letting him display the flag, learn patriotic music and see a parade, if possible. Such occasions may inspire him to draw or paint a picture that will illustrate his knowledge or feelings about his country.

Further study of anatomy and physiology is also appropriate at this age. Names of bones, muscles and nerves and their functions can be learned and their interdependence can be studied. Your child can understand how the health of the body affects the mind, and how proper mental attitudes (mental health) affect the body. He needs to know that the body is controlled by natural laws. It requires regular and sufficient sleep, exercise, sunshine, fresh air, water, and nutritious food. If he disobeys these laws, the result is illness or a weakened body. Such basic knowledge, solidly instilled throughout the early years, will help to provide a safeguard against unhealthful practices later on.

As he grows older, the child may, at times, be careless about how he eats or drinks or otherwise takes care of himself, but he is less likely to do so if he knows the consequences. Self-preservation is a strong instinct, and pride in a healthy mind and body will go a long way toward protecting your child against damaging habits.

If there is illness in the family, it usually puts an extra burden on the mother, but a child can be a great help in caring for a sick person. He can keep the water glass filled, bring juices or other food, comb the patient's hair, fluff the pillow, straighten the bedcovers, bring the mail or reading material and otherwise help the patient to be comfortable.

This is an excellent age to teach how to *prevent* illness. Your child should know the value of drinking water —at least four to six glasses daily, before or between meals —instead of soft drinks, and in addition to fruit juices and milk. He should understand his need for exercise, fresh air and sunshine and for regular bowel movements. And he can be taught to resort to natural remedies, where possible, instead of pills.

There are many things you can do both to prevent and to cure common illnesses—and you save money in the process.* When, for example, any member of the family has tonsillitis, is hoarse or feels a sore throat coming on, your child can learn how to put on a heating compress made from the simplest of materials. For example: Take two or three thicknesses of cotton cloth, perhaps from an old sheet; it should be about two inches wide and long enough to go around the neck twice. Wet it, wring it out so that it is wet but not dripping and wrap it comfortably snug around the neck. Then completely cover it with a wider piece of thick wool flannel and fasten securely with safety pins. A wool sock or a sleeve cut from an old wool sweater or other wool cloth will do. The patient should wear warm nightclothes, be warmly covered, have a warm drink of water with a little lemon juice in it or a Vitamin C tablet and go to sleep. In the morning, the neck should be sponged with a cold, wet cloth and promptly dried. This application of mild, moist heat to the affected part can be repeated nightly until the symptoms disappear.

The same type of treatment can be applied to a painful joint: to the abdomen in cases of indigestion, insomnia and constipation; and to the chest in cases of colds, flu, asthma, whooping cough, croup and similar problems. Of course, your physician should be your guide whenever there is any question.

A chest pack is especially effective in curing the night coughing so common with children who have had a cold for a day or so. Cough syrup relieves the symptoms but not the cause. A simple chest pack can be made from an old cotton T-shirt with the sleeves cut out, small enough

*These suggestions are from a section on Simple Home Treatments in the book *You and Your Health* by Harold Shryock, M.D. and Hubert O. Swartout, M.D., Doctors of Public Health in collaboration with 38 leading medical specialists. Vol. 3, pp. 303–324, 1970: Pacific Press Publishing Association, Mountain View, California. Library of Congress Card #69–10033.

to fit snugly to the person's chest area. It should be damp-
ened and wrung out before it is put on, then covered with
a tightly fitting sweater, pinning the neck and sleeves, if
necessary, taking care that the air cannot circulate under
the edges and cause chilling. For a very young baby, or a
very thin or old person, who may not have the natural
body warmth to heat up the moist pack, apply cam-
phorated oil or similar medication to the chest and use
only the dry covering.

For someone who has trouble going to sleep, a back
rub applied with even pressure and in a slow rhythm does
much to relax the muscles and quiet the nerves. Plain
talcum powder can be used to help the hands slide
smoothly over the body. A child will often enjoy giving
you a rub. He can also learn to give a hot foot bath—to
himself or another—after exposure to cold or dampness.
This is good insurance against catching a cold. The only
requirements are that the hot water in a pail or small tub
cover his ankles and that the water gradually be made as
hot as he can stand it. It is unlikely that anyone could
tolerate a temperature hot enough to be unsafe. After
between five and 30 minutes, the feet should be dashed
with cold water and briskly rubbed dry. A cold, wet cloth
on the forehead will forestall any faintness as the heat
draws blood from other parts of the body.

Such treatments should, of course, be supervised by
a responsible person until your child becomes skillful in
giving them. One of the best sources of information for
basic health care is the latest Red Cross book on *home
nursing*. Many nurses and physicians are willing to familiarize groups of parents and children with the lessons in
this book, without charging for the service.

And now, finally, your child is ready for school. When
he is 8 to 10 years old, his vision, hearing, brain and gen-

eral physical constitution are well enough developed so that a reasonable school program is not too demanding. If he has not been previously frustrated by demands beyond his ability, he will respond eagerly to a more formal education. He is now equipped to absorb knowledge. He has been learning to reason from cause to effect and is capable of other abstract thinking. He can now discriminate between reality and fantasy and is also ready cheerfully to spend several hours a day away from home and family. He has a natural inclination to be a member of a group and to identify with others of his age and sex. His chance of succeeding in the usual school subjects is almost 100%.

It should be noted again, at this point, that most children who start school late should not be started in the first grade. Assuming reasonably good parenting, they should be started as many grades later as the number of years they delayed school entrance. So the typical 7-year-old may start in the second grade and the 8-year-old in the third. There is no set rule here. The child's social and emotional maturity must be considered. But he should not be held out a year, or two or three and then started in the first grade to go lock-step through all the grades, out of step with his age group.

The ideal school situation for the later entrant is, of course, the nongraded school. Given reasonably good rearing along lines suggested in this book, within a few weeks or months, he will catch up with the earlier entrants. His maturity and stability will be better than the average. And the discerning teacher will quickly recognize his potential and fill in any of the gaps in his learning. She will find him an asset to her class.

Because of the child's relative maturity, ages 8–10 are usually considered to be the ideal time for remedial work if he started school at 6 and failed, or if he has shown physical or psychological distress. As we have stressed, it is much better to give children rich experiences at home until they are really ready for formal reading, writing and arithmetic. Even those children who begin school at 6 and do manage to have success certainly would not be harmed by a few more years in an unstructured home or homelike environment. And while the damage done to this group by the usual school routine may not be so noticeable as the scholastic failure of the others, eye defects, emotional weaknesses, loss of motivation and other difficulties often develop later. These are seldom traced to one of their most certain sources—schooling or unnecessary care out of the home before the child has reached his integrated maturity level at around ages 8–10. Since, at present, there is no sure way of predicting success or failure in school, the only safe way to avoid damage to the child's development is to delay schooling until the IML is reached.

Summary and Recommendations

Until recently, there has been a hesitancy to question the strong movement toward universal early schooling. Many school administrators who have had reservations have felt that the movement had such power and had gone so far that it could not be stopped. But some of these men and women now are beginning to share their findings and to pay more attention to research evidence before they move ahead with their planning. Nevertheless, leaders in certain states and local areas are continuing to urge earlier and earlier schooling and, in some cases, earlier mandatory school-entrance-age laws.

It is time that human ecology be given the kind of attention that, for the last few years, has been directed toward our environment. We all have heard the ecologist's message: We cannot continue to live as we do if we are to have a livable world. The same determination must be applied to our children: We must change our approach to their early education or we will not have stable, well-motivated and happy children.

In their best-selling book, *Blueprint for Survival,* the editors of *The Ecologist* come to some penetrating conclusions, which they base on the recent Report of the Study of Critical Environmental Problems issued in 1970 by the Massachusetts Institute of Technology. They say:

> Industrial man in the world today is like a bull in a china shop, with the single difference that a bull with half the information about the properties of china as we have about those of ecosystems would probably try to adapt its behavior to its environment rather than the reverse. By contrast, *Homo sapiens industrialis* is determined that the china shop should adapt to him, and has therefore set himself the goal of reducing it to rubble in the shortest possible time.

We have no delusions that it will be easy to reverse these inclinations insofar as they relate to early childhood education. As Robert Heilbroner (66) has said, "Little is gained when we delude ourselves as to the ease with which human society can be restructured." Yet we agree with him that ". . . the cause of reform, not to mention that of constructive revolution, is too important to be nurtured on anything but the truth." We must patiently but courageously deal with a wide and complex circle of individuals and organizations if we are to affect any ECE reform or revolution.

Educators, psychologists, sociologists, pediatricians, politicians, neurologists, publishers, toy makers, and teachers associations not to mention parents, have a stake in the young child. Some are fighting one another, others are trying to cooperate with one another. When the researcher enters the picture, he cannot possibly please all. They may not even allow him to explain. And sometimes, he has not explained clearly when he has had the chance. Or, he has not bothered to relate his findings to fellow researchers. So there is confusion and verbal cannibalism about ECE.

Meanwhile, those who hold the purse strings—or hope to—move on in what seems to be the expedient way, sometimes right, sometimes very wrong. Sometimes, they have little concern for the voice of research even when there is remarkable agreement among researchers. The result is planning and legislation for ECE based more on tradition and intuition, than on documented findings.

In industry, when planners ignore researchers, the result often is an unacceptable product. Yet too many ECE planners and legislators ignore research when they plan projects. Only they are experimenting with your youngsters. They often find sound research findings to be unpalatable, to interfere with their private ideas; as a result, they risk the welfare of children at gross costs to the family, not to mention the taxpayer. Even more unfortunately, the possible effects of their errors are not so clearly measurable or subject to control as the manufacture of drugs or aircraft brakes, for example.

Early childhood specialists are becoming increasingly aware of these risks. We have mentioned prominent clinicians and researchers who once strongly advocated early schooling or day care as generally desirable for young children, but who now believe that the home is the best place for early education whenever possible. Nor, contrary to common assumptions, do most school administrators agree that day care or early schooling should be provided for all children.

Many teachers agree that early schooling may be

harmful. Queenie Cales (22), a California remedial reading teacher who specializes in working with the emotionally handicapped, writes, "I spend half of my life telling people if they want to put me out of a job, start sending kids (boys at least) to school after age seven."

Early-schooling advocates who believe they have the endorsement of the great majority of young people should look again. Lisa Blumberg, a junior at Wellesley College, summarizes the feelings of many who have written us:

> In my psychology courses, I read case histories of psychopaths, chronic "losers" and individuals who are totally dependent on drugs. One thing that most of these people have in common is they suffered from parental neglect, when they were children. In very many cases their parents were not overtly abusive to them, they were just inattentive or absent for prolonged periods.
>
> I would like to see the government paying a substantial sum to women to take care of their preschoolers since I think this would be better for the children and thus for the country than setting up a vast network of day care centers.
>
> . . .Women must be liberated but it must not be at the expense of children. No woman should feel that she must have a child if she does not sincerely want one. However if she voluntarily decides to have one, there are certain sacrifices she should strongly be encouraged to make. One of these is staying home with the child until he is of school age.
>
> Every worthwhile thing one does whether it is going to college, serving in the peace corps, etc., involves giving up a block of time to concentrate on that one thing, and parenthood is no exception. I think most women really are not opposed to giving up full-time jobs when their children are young, but now the pressures of society and expectations seem to be against women choosing to be full-time

mothers for a while. I hope society will soon realize again that housewifery for those who want it can be creative, fulfilling and exciting.

It is commonly known that most care centers and preschools simply do not have enough staff with enough time to give enough attention to their charges. Yet certain states insist on providing care for all children regardless of need, even though they are not able to provide adequate care even for those who *are* in need. Ohio legislators, (112) for example, in 1972, voted the following maximums for the number of children per staff member in care centers:

Under 18 months	8
Eighteen months to under 3 years	10
Three to under 5 years	15
Five years and older	20

How much love and warmth can be provided on a one-to-one basis by one person who is responsible for eight or ten infants? And what person can responsively care for 15 three-year-olds?

Many authorities now believe that a lack of warm, consistent, responsive care in the home during the developmental years has contributed to the increasing incidence of juvenile crime and other delinquency in recent years. If children do not build a sense of self-worth through responsibility in the home, when and where are they going to build it? If they do not develop a sound value system through operating on a personal, one-to-one basis in the home, what assurance do they have of ever developing it? Day care or early schooling will fill the void only when the home situation is impossible or nonexistent and even then only in a limited way.

We have pointed out the results of placing a child under influences that parents cannot control, of tossing him into a competition for attention that often he cannot handle. We have noted how he turns from his parents to his peers for his standards and how he learns not so much how to be sociable as how to conform. We have shown how he becomes frustrated and anxiety-ridden when he is asked to read before he can see, or hear or comprehend adequately. We have seen how he turns off the whole process, how he rebels. And the little child who becomes lost in the demands and counterdemands of an unstable society becomes the citizen and the parent of the future.

We have noted that research has come up with scant evidence for lasting benefits for most children from early schooling. On the other hand, scientific evidence impressively favors later school admission. Studies have shown that, among early starters, there is a greater likelihood of regression or loss of motivation as the years pass, while the late starters appear, generally, to thrive and excel mentally, emotionally and socially. They excel in achievement, motivation, leadership and behavior.

At present, most education is based upon an ability to read. And as reading specialist Nila Smith points out, "Dozens of investigations indicate that reading maturation accompanies physical growth, mental growth, emotional and social maturity, experiential background and language development." Yet in spite of all of this evidence, some leading educators still say that the concept of readiness is outmoded. The colt does not become ready for racing by trying before he is able to; nor does the mother kangaroo urge her baby to hop before he is ready. It is the same with children. Says Ethelouise Carpenter, professor of early childhood education at Kent State University:

Children are constantly involved in different degrees of readiness. They are called to meals and they linger; they are put on their feet to walk and they plop down on the floor. There are signs for being ready and for not being ready. The state of readiness has not come about through practice of the things to come but through a maturing process fed by successions of related experiences. A child does not become ready for walking by walking. When all elements are perfectly coordinated he begins to walk and he perfects this skill over a long period of time.

Many people have come to look upon readiness as something that must happen to children during the spring preceding first grade!

The question is not only, "Is the child ready for school?" but even more important, "Will the early starter be as well or better motivated and less frustrated and anxiety-ridden as the one who starts later?"

We do not blame earnest parents for being concerned about the mental alertness of their children in their early years. The child must not be reared in an environment barren of intellectual stimulation. But he must be free and feel warmth and security, and the home most often can satisfy these needs if the suggestions in the previous chapters are reasonably followed.

Nor should parents be greatly concerned about Benjamin Bloom's assertion that half the child's intellectual capacity is attained by age 4 and an additional 30% by his eighth year. As David Elkind points out, this does not mean that if he does not learn certain things early, he will not learn them later. The fact is, he will probably learn better later.

Some suggest that geniuses generally have been stimulated early. But Elkind notes that this does not mean that early stimulation contributed to the genius or advanced it. There is reason to believe that many such individuals would have been even more productive and less neurotic if they had enjoyed a less-pressured early child-hood.

But is a preschool any worse than a large family? This question is asked both by sincere parents and by critics who note our insistence on small adult-to-child ratios. The answer is that preschool in most cases *is* worse. Children in preschools are about the same age and come from widely diverse home backgrounds. And they are insecure because they have been taken out of the nest. However, in large families, the children are of different ages and, with reasonable parental direction, are more able and likely to help than to compete with one another. And whatever problems do arise, the children have the security of the home.

Parents in favor of preschool should consider whether they are being consistent. The very parent who worries over his child for the first few years for fear he may be injured or wrongly influenced, will ship him off to preschool with little hesitation or concern about his mental, moral or physical safety. No wonder that many children are hurt by the ignorance and callousness of their parents.

The larger issue, then, is not, "Shall my child go to nursery school?" but, "Who shall control the mind and thoughts of my developing child? Shall the family remain as the basic unit of our society? How long will our culture survive without the family?"

It is time for citizens to demand education in parenting and family care more than early schooling. They should insist on responsible school-entrance-age legislation that recognizes the facts of child development and provides latitude for family convictions. They should see that services are provided for the poor, the deprived and the handicapped without insisting on those services for themselves.

The poor also need a fair ECE assessment. They too

must have the right to choose how their children should be reared. Social worker Sheila Rothman notes that ". . . many [public] officials find the idea of day care especially appealing" and set out to take the control of children from their mothers. She declares, "No one reads women liberationist rhetoric on day care with greater glee than relief administrators." Rothman based some of her conclusions on a national study of 500 public day-care centers conducted by the National Council of Jewish Women in 1972, (84) which cited the mediocre or low quality of care in most centers, the futility of licensing them and the difficulty in finding and keeping quality day-care personnel. Rothman urges that payments be made to the poor so that mothers can take care of their own children—a system that would be cheaper than hiring day-care "professionals."

John Bowlby agrees with this idea of mothers caring for their own children whenever possible. And he makes a further practical suggestion:

> I strongly favour setting up mothers' clubs to which lonely mothers can come as and when they like, but especially in the early afternoons, where they will meet with others and make friends, and also make arrangements for mutual aid, and where their very young children will have a chance to meet with a few others *in the presence of their mothers.* In my view a club of this sort should be run, not by a professional person, but by one or more motherly women who themselves have children and who are familiar at first hand with the kinds of problems mothers of young children are likely to be facing. Whilst that is the basic qualification, there would be no harm in their having some knowledge of child development as well, but I would regard that as secondary. (17)

Of course, there are many services that can, and should, be provided for all, some of them publicly, others privately. For instance, while we do not suggest that our public agencies move into a full-blown program of social-ized medicine, we do believe that every child should be afforded at least minimal medical care to insure his sound physical, mental and emotional growth. For many fami-lies, much of this care is already provided by the family physician, supplemented by Public Health agencies. For the rest, special provision should be made for diagnostic services, as well as for innoculations and other Public Health services that are generally taken for granted in our country today.

In research on ECE, more than casual attention should be paid to the integrated maturity level (IML) concept. The fact that maturity in so many child-develop-ment areas is reached at about the same time in the child's life should impress parents, legislators and ECE people alike. These areas include neurophysiology, cognition, vi-sion, hearing, intersensory perception and socio-emo-tional development. And the importance of their relative maturity to success in school is underscored by nearly all studies that have compared ages at school entrance with performance. There is virtually no replicated evidence that favors taking a youngster from an adequate home and placing him in the care of others before he is 8 to 10 or 11—when he has reached his IML. And boys will al-most always reach this level later than girls, which makes most school-entrance laws even more unfair to boys.

We hesitate to add another burden to an already top-heavy bureaucracy, but we feel impelled to suggest that the Congress and the President study the possibility of establishing a National Commission on the Home and Family. We urge that more mothers reevaluate their "need" to work, especially in view of the increasing costs for day care and for household help. We suggest that business and industry consider offering half-day employ-ment for mothers who feel that they must work, yet who are determined to fulfill their family obligations better than they can if employed full time.

It is also time for the states to review their school entrance age laws. No states that require school entrance at 5 and 6 for *all* children are being fair to them, especially to boys who at the same age are generally six to twelve months less mature than little girls.

Awakening parents to an awareness of the primacy of their children's needs is perhaps the greatest educational challenge of the decade. If the challenge is met, we might find that until they are 8 years old, as many as 60–70% of our children will be reared in their own homes—by their own parent or parents—with little exposure to television and academics but with much freedom, friendship and responsibility. Of those who do not or cannot remain at home, a relatively few privileged youngsters will be adopted by surrogate parents. Others will be placed in family day care, in foster homes with motherly women who are charged with the care of no more than five children each. Sheila Rothman suggests the establishment of child-care registries of mothers who have successfully reared families, much like the nurses' registries so common today. If the mothers were found unsuited, they would simply be removed from the registries.

Until provision can be made for the remaining children who do not fit into one of the above categories, they should be placed in the best possible nursery schools or care centers, in which activities are provided along the lines suggested in earlier chapters of this book.

If ECE planners will use their teachers to give parent education a try, and if legislators will, for the moment, turn aside vested interests and pressure groups, a new day will dawn for young children. Parenthood will be strengthened more than questioned. As parents learn, they will enjoy their children more and will allow them to mature before having to meet the pressures of school. And for both parents and children, as Ralph Waldo Emerson suggested, the years will teach much that the days never knew.

Acknowledgment

We leaned heavily on a large number of professionals in preparing this book. Principal among these were Dr. Martha Lorenz, Hewitt Research Foundation family specialist; Dennis Moore, Hewitt Research Associate; Dr. Herald Habenicht, consulting pediatrician of Andrews University; Dr. David Metcalf, child psychiatrist and neurophysiologist of the University of Colorado School of Medicine; and the staff of the ERIC/ECE Center at Urbana, Illinois. Our manuscript preparation was skillfully supervised by Mrs. Shirley Swensen.

Many ECE leaders, researchers and clinicians were especially encouraging or helpful to us. Among them are some of the nation's and world's leading ECE scholars. However, in acknowledging their help, we accept full responsibility for the conclusions we present. We do not in any case suggest that they are responsible for our conclusions nor that they necessarily agree with all of them.

We do, however, express our gratitude to these psychologists, psychiatrists, neurophysiologists, legislators, and others who are students or shapers of early childhood policy. They include among still others Mary Ainsworth, Milton Akers, Millie Almy, Sueann Ambron, Louise Ames, Jean Ayers, Bernell Baldwin, Nancy Bayley, Silvia Bell, Carl Bereiter, the late Herbert Birch, Lisa Blumberg, John Bowlby, John Brademas, Urie Bronfenbrenner, Jere Brophy, James Buckley, Leon Burros, Bettye Caldwell, Don Clausen, Lois-ellen Datta, Ronald Davie, Paul Dokecki, Malcolm Douglass, David Elkind, Martin Engel, Sigfried Engelmann, Fernando Esteves, Pascal Forgione, Hans Furth, Ira Gordon, Margaret Gott, Edith Green, Edith Grotberg, Joseph Halliwell, Darrell Harmon, Emily Harris, Robert Hess, Henry Hilgartner, Marjorie Honzik, Torsten Husen, Frances Ilg, Bärbel Inhelder, Jerome Kagan, Lillian Katz, Robert Kraskin, Catherine Landreth, Phyllis Levenstein, Robert Liljefors, Walter MacGinitie, Eve Malmquist, George Mayeske, Margaret Mead, Dale Meers, George Milkie, Walter Mondale, Robert Moon, Humberto Nagera, Frank Newton, Glen Nimnicht, Earl Ogletree, Jean Piaget, Anneliese Pokrandt, Anneliese Pontius, Albert Quie, Helen and U. D. Register, William Rohwer, Jerome Rosner, Sally Ryan, Earl Schaefer, Karl Schaefer, William Shannon, Alberta Siegel, Norman Silberberg, René Spitz, Uve Stave, Robert Strom, Priscilla Travis, Gilbert Voyat, David Weikert, Burton White, Sheldon White, Joseph Willey, Morvin Wirtz, Paul Yakovlev, Ethel Young, Francis Young and Edward Zigler.

Bibliography

1. AINSWORTH, MARY D. *et al.* "The Effects of Maternal Deprivation: A Review of Findings and Controversy in the Context of Research Strategy." *Deprivation of Maternal Care, a Reassessment of its Effects.* New York: Shocken Books, 1967, pp. 289–351.

2. AKERS, MILTON. Letter to R. S. Moore, November 17, 1972.

3. ALMY, MILLIE. *et al. Young Children's Thinking.* New York: Teachers College, Columbia University, 1966.

4. AMES, LOUISE B. *Is Your Child in the Wrong Grade?* New York: Harper & Row, 1967.

5. _____. *Stop School Failure.* New York: Harper & Row, 1972.

6. AYRES, A. JEAN. "Reading—a Product of Sensory Integrative Processes." *Perception and Reading.* Helen K. Smith, ed. Newark, Delaware: International Reading Association, 1968, pp. 77–82.

7. BARBRACK, CHRISTOPHER R., and DELLA M. HORTON. *Educational Intervention in the Home and Paraprofessional Ca-*

218

reer Development. DARCEE Papers and Reports, vol. 4, no. 4. Nashville: Peabody College, July 1970.

8. BARTLETT, VIRGIL. Conversation with R. S. Moore, December 3, 1973.

9. BAYLEY, NANCY. "Development of Mental Abilities." *Carmichael's Manual of Child Psychology*, vol. I. John Mussen, ed. New York: Wiley & Sons, 1970, pp. 1163–1209.

10. BELL, SILVIA. *Early Cognitive Development and Its Relationship to Infant-Mother Attachment: A Study of Disadvantaged Negro Infants*. U. S. Department of Health, Education and Welfare, November 1971.

11. BERGER, ALLAN S. "Anxiety in Young Children." *Young Children*, October 1971, pp. 5–11.

12. BIRCH, H. G. and A. LEFFORD. "Intersensory Development in Children." *Monograph of the Society for Research in Child Development*, #89, 1963.

13. BLATT, BURTON and FRANK GARFUNKEL. *The Education of Intelligence*. Washington, D.C.: The Council for Exceptional Children, 1969.

14. BLOOM, BENJAMIN S. *Stability and Change in Human Characteristics*. New York: Wiley & Sons, 1964.

15. BLUMBERG, LISA. Letter to R. S. Moore, July 23, 1972.

16. BOWLBY, JOHN. *Attachment and Loss, Vol. II, Separation: Anxiety and Anger*. New York: Basic Books, 1973.

17. ———. Letters to R. S. Moore, December 18, 1972, and October 25, 1973.

18. ———. *Maternal Care and Mental Health*. Geneva: World Health Organization, 1952.

19. BRIGHAM, AMARIAH. *Remarks on the Influence of Mental Cultivation and Mental Excitement upon Health*. Hartford: F. J. Huntington, 1832.

20. BRONFENBRENNER, URIE. *Is Early Intervention Effective?* Unpublished Manuscript. Cornell University, 1973.

21. BRUNER, JEROME. *The Process of Education*. Cambridge: Harvard University Press, 1960.

22. CALES, QUEENIE. Letter to R. S. Moore, November 25, 1973.

23. California State Task Force Report. *Report of the Task Force on Early Childhood Education*, Wilson Riles, State Superintendent of Public Instruction and The State Board of Education, November 26, 1971.

24. ———. *Report of the Task Force on Early Childhood Education*,

Wilson Riles, State Superintendent of Public Instruction and The State Board of Education, June 1972.

25. CARPENTER, ETHELOUISE. "Readiness is Being." *Childhood Education*, November 1961, pp. 57–59.

26. CARTER, LOWELL B. "The Effect of Early School Entrance on the Scholastic Achievement of Elementary School Children in the Austin Public Schools." *Journal of Educational Research*, vol. 50 (October 1956), 91–103.

27. CHALFANT, JAMES C. and MARGARET A. SCHEFFELIN. *Central Processing Dysfunctions in Children: A Review of Research*. NINDS Monograph #9. U. S. Department of Health, Education and Welfare, 1969.

28. CLARK, ALBERT. Conversation with R. S. Moore, September 22, 1973.

29. COLE, LUELLA. *The Improvement of Reading and Special Reference to Remedial Instruction*. New York: Farrar & Rinehart, 1938.

30. COLEMAN, H. M. "Visual Perception and Reading Dysfunction." *Journal of Learning Disabilities*, February 1968, pp. 116–123.

31. COMBS, ARTHUR W., editor. *Perceiving, Behaving, Becoming*, Washington, D.C.: Association for Supervision and Curriculum Development, 1965.

32. CORBIN, PENUEL H. Thesis submitted to the Faculty of the Graduate School, University of Minnesota, for Master of Science Degree in Pediatrics, June 1951.

33. DAVIE, RONALD, NEVILLE BUTLER and HARVEY GOLDSTEIN. *From Birth to Seven*. New York: Longmans, Green, 1972.

34. DAVIS, H. M. "Don't Push Your School Beginners." *Parent's Magazine*, vol. 27 (October 1952), 140–141.

35. DEWEY, JOHN. "The Primary Education Fetich." *Forum*, vol. 25, 1898.

36. DOUGLASS, MALCOLM P. *Innovation and the Credibility Gap*. Address to California Elementary School Administrators Association and the California Association for Supervision and Curriculum Development, Palo Alto, January 19, 1968.

37. EAGAN, WALTER. Letter to Wilson Riles, April 25, 1973.

38. Educational Policies Commission of the NEA and the American Association of School Administrators. "Universal Opportunity for Early Childhood Education." *NEA Journal*, November 1966, pp. 8–10, 12.

39. ELKIND, DAVID. "The Case for the Academic Preschool: Fact or

Fiction?" *Young Children*, vol. XXV, no. 3 (January 1970), 132–140.

40. ———. "Early Childhood Education: A Piagetian Perspective." *National Elementary School Principal*, September 1971, pp. 28–31.

41. ———. "Piagetian and Psychometric Conceptions of Intelligence." *Harvard Educational Review*, vol. 39 (Spring 1969), 319–337.

42. ENGEL, MARTIN. *The Care and Feeding of Children for Fun and Profit*. Unpublished manuscript, National Demonstration Center in Early Childhood Education, U. S. Office of Education. No date, (a).

43. ———. *Rapunzel, Rapunzel, Let Down Your Golden Hair*. Unpublished manuscript, National Demonstration Center in Early Childhood Education, U. S. Office of Education. No date, (b).

44. FISHER, JAMES T., and LOWELL S. HAWLEY. *A Few Buttons Missing*. Philadelphia: Lippincott, 1951.

45. FORESTER, JOHN J. "At What Age Should Children Start School?" *School Executive*, vol. 74 (March 1955), 80, 81.

46. FROSTIG, M. "Visual Modality, Research and Practice." *Perception and Reading*. Helen K. Smith, ed. Newark, Delaware: International Reading Association, 1968, pp. 25–33.

47. FURTH, HANS G. *Piaget for Teachers*. Englewood Cliffs, N.J.: Prentice-Hall, 1970.

48. GEBER, MARCELLE. "The Psycho-Motor Development of African Children in the First Year, and the Influence of Maternal Behavior." *Journal of Social Psychology*, vol. 47 (1958), 185–195.

49. GESELL, ARNOLD. *The Normal Child and Primary Education*. New York: Ginn & Co., 1912.

50. ———, and Ilg, Frances L. *The Child from Five to Ten*. New York: Harper & Brothers, 1946.

51. ———. *The Infant and Child in the Culture of Today*. New York: Harper & Brothers, 1943.

52. GOLDSMITH, EDWARD *et al. Blueprint for Survival*. Boston: Houghton Mifflin Co., 1972.

53. GOTT, MARGARET E. *The Effect of Age Difference at Kindergarten Entrance on Achievement and Adjustment in Elementary School*. Unpublished doctoral dissertation, University of Colorado, 1963.

54. GRAMLICH, SAM. Conversation with R. S. Moore, November 28, 1973.

55. GRAY, LILLIAN. *Teaching Children to Read.* 3rd ed. New York: Ronald Press, 1963.

56. GRAY, SUSAN W. "Children from Three to Ten: The Early Training Project." *Longitudinal Evaluations of Preschool Programs.* Sally Ryan, ed. Washington, D.C.: Office of Child Development. 1974.

57. ———. "The Child's First Teacher." *Childhood Education,* December 1971, pp. 127–129.

58. ———. *Selected Longitudinal Studies of Compensatory Education—A Look from the Inside.* Nashville: George Peabody College, 1969.

59. GROTBERG, EDITH H., ed. *Day Care: Resources for Decisions.* Washington, D.C.: Office of Economic Opportunity, 1971.

60. GUMPERT, DAVID. "Unequal Rights." Wall Street Journal, March 22, 1972, pp. 1, 17.

61. HALL, R. VANCE. "Does Entrance Age Affect Achievement?" *Elementary School Journal,* April 1963, pp. 396–399.

62. HALLIWELL, JOSEPH W. "Reviewing the Reviews on Entrance Age and School Success." *Journal of Educational Research,* vol. 59 (May–June 1966), 395–401.

63. ———, and Belle W. Stein. "A Comparison of the Achievement of Early and Late Starters in Reading Related and Non-Reading Related Areas in Fourth and Fifth Grades." *Elementary English,* October 1964, pp. 631–639, 658.

64. HEBER, RICK and HOWARD GARBER. *An Experiment in the Prevention of Cultural Familial Mental Retardation.* Paper presented at the Second Congress of the International Association for Scientific Study of Mental Deficiency, August–September 1970.

65. HEFFERNAN, HELEN. "A Vital Curriculum for Today's Young Child." *Early Childhood Education Rediscovered.* Joe L. Frost, ed. New York: Holt, Rinehart and Winston, Inc., 1968, pp. 491–497.

66. HEILBRONER, ROBERT. *In the Name of Profit: Profiles in Corporate Irresponsibility.* New York: Doubleday & Co., 1972.

67. HELMORE, G. A. *Piaget, A Practical Consideration.* Elmsford, N.Y.: Pergamon Press, 1969.

68. HENDRICKSON, H. "The Vision Development Process." *Visual and Perceptual Aspects for the Achieving and Underachiev-*

ing Child. Robert M. Wold, ed. Seattle: Special Child Publications, 1969, pp. 1–10.

69. HESS, R. D., *et al.* "Parent Involvement in Early Education," and "Parent Training Programs and Community Involvement in Day Care." *Day Care: Resources for Decision.* Edith H. Grotberg, ed. Washington, D.C.: Office of Economic Opportunity, 1971, pp. 265–312.

70. HESS, R. D., and VIRGINIA SHIPMAN. "Maternal Attitudes Toward the School and the Role of Pupil: Some Social Class Comparisons." *Developing Programs for the Educationally Disadvantaged.* A. Harry Passow, ed. New York: Teachers College, Columbia University, 1968, pp. 2–3.

71. HILGARTNER, HENRY L. *The Frequency of Myopia in Individuals Under 21 Years of Age.* Paper presented to the Texas Medical Society, Austin, Texas, 1962.

72. _____. Letter to R. S. Moore, June 30, 1972.

73. HOFFMAN, BETTY H. "Do You Know How to Play with your Child?" *Woman's Day,* August 1972, pp. 46, 118–120.

74. HUSEN, TORSTEN, ed. *International Study of Achievement in Mathematics,* vol. II. New York: John Wiley, 1967.

75. ILG, FRANCES L., and LOUISE B. AMES. "Developmental Trends in Reading Behavior." *Journal of Genetic Psychology,* June 1950, pp. 291–311.

76. ISRAELI TEACHER. Documented interview with R. S. Moore, October 1973.

77. JENCKS, CRISTOPHER S. "The Coleman Report and the Conventional Wisdom." *On Equality of Educational Opportunity.* Frederick Mosteller and Daniel P. Moynihan, eds. New York: Random House, 1972, pp. 37–42.

78. JENSEN, ARTHUR R. "How Much Can We Boost IQ and Scholastic Achievement?" *Harvard Educational Review,* vol. 39 (Winter 1969), 1–123.

79. JOHNSON, R. H. "Parent and Child Centers, Early Intervention." *Head Start Newsletter,* December–January, 1972–1973, pp. 1–9.

80. KAGAN, JEROME. *Cross Cultural Perspectives on Early Development.* Paper presented at the American Association for the Advancement of Science, December 26, 1972.

81. _____. "Inadequate Evidence and Illogical Conclusions." *Harvard Educational Review,* vol. 39 (Spring 1969), 274–277.

82. _____. "On Class Differences and Early Development." *Educa-*

tion of the Infant and Young Child. Victor H. Denenberg, ed. New York: Academic Press, 1970, pp. 10–15.

83. ———, and Phillip Whitten. "Day Care Can Be Dangerous." *Psychology Today,* December 1970, pp. 37–39.

84. KEYSERLING, MARY DUBLIN. *Windows on Day Care.* New York: National Council of Jewish Women, 1972.

85. KING, INEZ B. "Effect of Age of Entrance into Grade I Upon Achievement in Elementary School." *Elementary School Journal,* vol. 55 (February 1955), 331–36.

86. KLAUS, MARSHALL H., and J. H. KENNELL. "Mothers Separated from Their Newborn Infants." *Pediatric Clinics of North America,* November 1970, pp. 1015–37.

87. KRIPPNER, STANLEY. Address to 21st Annual School Vision Forum and Reading Conference, 1968.

88. LAIRY, G. C. et al. *E.E.G. and Clinical Neurophysiology,* vol. 14 (1962), 778–779.

89. LEONARD, GEORGE B. *Education and Ecstasy.* New York: Dell Publishing Company, 1968.

90. LEVENSTEIN, PHYLLIS. "Learning Through (and from) Mothers." *Childhood Education,* vol. 48, no. 3 (December 1971), 130–134.

91. LOW, SETH and PEARL SPINDLER. *Child Care Arrangements of Working Mothers in the United States.* Washington, D.C.: Children's Bureau Publication No. 46, 1968.

92. Massachusetts Institute of Technology. *Man's Impact on the Total Environment,* Report of the Study of Critical Environmental Problems. Boston, 1970.

93. MAWHINNEY, PAUL E. "We Gave Up on Early Entrance." *Michigan Education Journal,* May, 1964.

94. MAY, DEAN, and MARIS VINOVSKIS. *A Ray of Millenial Light: Early Education and Social Reform in the Infant School Movement in Massachusetts, 1826–1840.* Paper presented at the Clark University Conference on Family and Social Structure, April 22, 1972.

95. MAYESKE, GEORGE. *On the Explanation of Racial-Ethnic Group Differences in Achievement Test Scores.* Washington, D.C.: U. S. Office of Education. No date.

96. MEERS, DALE. Statement in *Head Start, Child Development Legislation,* Senate Bill 3193. Hearing before the Subcommittee on Children and Youth and the Subcommittee on Employment, Manpower and Poverty. Washington, D.C., March 27, 1972 (a).

97. ———. Letter to R. S. Moore, August 20, 1972 (b).

98. MEIERHOFER, MARIE. In *Today's Child,* May 1972, p. 5.

99. METCALF, DAVID R. Letter to R. S. Moore, March 22, 1974.

100. ———, and KENT JORDAN. "EEG Ontogenesis in Normal Children." *Drugs, Development, and Cerebral Function.* W. Lynn Smith, ed. Springfield, Illinois: Charles C. Thomas, 1972, pp. 125–144.

101. MILKIE, GEORGE. Letter to R. S. Moore, October 13, 1972.

102. MOORE, RAYMOND S. *Experiment in Work Education for Children.* Unpublished report of experimental studies in elementary schools, 1960.

103. ———, and DENNIS R. MOORE. "Early Schooling for All?" *The Congressional Record,* vol. 118, no. 167 (October 16, 1972a), E8726–E8740.

104. ———. "The Race to the Schoolhouse." *Harper's Magazine,* July 1972b.

105. MORENCY, ANNE. "Auditory Modality and Reading." *Perception and Reading.* Helen K. Smith, ed. Newark, Delaware: International Reading Association, 1968, pp. 17–20.

106. NAGERA, HUMBERTO. *Day Care Centers: Red Light, Green Light or Amber Light.* Unpublished manuscript, Ann Arbor: University of Michigan, 1972.

107. *Nation's Schools.* Opinion poll. January 1973, p. 78.

108. NELSON, W. E. *Textbook of Pediatrics.* Chicago: Saunders, 1967.

109. New York State Regents. *Prekindergarten Education,* a position paper. Albany, N.Y.: The State Education Department, December 1967.

110. NEWTON, FRANK H. Letter to R. S. Moore, October 24, 1972.

111. Office of Economic Opportunity. *State School Entrance Age Laws.* A study by Pascal Forgione in progress at the Stanford University School of Education. Directed by R. S. Moore and M. Kirst, Stanford, California, 1974.

112. Ohio. House Bill No. 81, 1972; House Bill No. 510, 1973.

113. OLSON, WILLARD C. "Experiences for Growing." *NEA Journal,* vol. 36 (October 1947), 502–503.

114. PHILLIP, JOHN L. *The Origins of Intellect, Theory.* San Francisco: H. W. Freeman, 1969.

115. PIAGET, JEAN. "Foreword" in *Young Children's Thinking* by M. Almy, E. Chittendon, and P. Miller. New York: Teachers College, Columbia University, 1966, pp. iii–vii.

116. ———. "The Stages of the Intellectual Development of the

Child." *Bulletin of the Menninger Clinic*, vol. 26, no. 3 (1962), 120–145.

117. POLLACK, JACK H. "A Startling New Study by the Gesell Institute: Is Your Child in the Wrong Grade?" *The Washington Post*, September 20, 1964, p. 4–5.

118. PONTIUS, ANNELIESE A. "Neurological Aspects in Some Type of Delinquency, Especially in Juvenile Form." *Adolescence*, Fall 1972, pp. 289–308.

119. RICH, DOROTHY. In "Phone Directory and Blue Jeans." *Sunday Star and Daily News* (Washington), May 6, 1973 and personal interview with R. Moore, March 20, 1973.

120. RILES, WILSON. *The Early Childhood Education Program Proposal.* Sacramento: California State Department of Education, 1972.

121. ROBINSON, MEREDITH L. *Compensatory Education and Early Adolescence.* Unpublished manuscript. Stanford Research Institute, 1973.

122. ROHWER, WILLIAM D. *Improving Instruction in the 1970's— What Can Make A Significant Difference?* Address to the American Educational Research Association, 1973.

123. _____. "Prime Time for Education: Early Childhood or Adolescence?" *Harvard Educational Review*, August 1971, pp. 316–341.

124. ROSENZWEIG, MARK R., EDWARD L. BENNETT and MARIAN C. DIAMOND. "Brain Changes in Response to Experience." *Scientific American*, February 1972, pp. 22–29.

125. ROSNER, JEROME. "Language Arts and Arithmetic Achievement, and Specifically Related Perceptual Skills." *American Educational Research Journal*, Winter 1973, 59–68.

126. ROTHMAN, SHEILA M. "Liberating Day Care: A Modest Proposal." *Phi Delta Kappan*, October 1973, pp. 132–135.

127. RYAN, SALLY., ed. *A Report on Longitudinal Evaluation of Preschool Programs.* Washington, D.C.: Office of Child Development, 1974.

128. SATO, TIKASI. *Acquired Myopia.* Address to the First International Conference on Myopia. New York: Myopia Research Foundation, September 1964.

129. SCHAEFER, EARL S. "Learning from Each Other." *Childhood Education*, October 1971a, pp. 3–7.

130. _____. "Parents as Educators: Evidence from Cross-Sectional, Longitudinal and Intervention Research." *Young Children*, April 1972, pp. 227–239.

131. ———. "Toward a Revolution in Education: A Perspective from Child Development Research." *National Elementary Principal*, September 1971b, pp. 18–25.

132. SHANNON, WILLIAM V. "A Radical, Direct, Simple, Utopian Alternative to Day-Care Centers." *New York Times Magazine*, April 30, 1972, editorial.

133. SILBERBERG, NORMAN, and MARGARET C. SILBERBERG, eds. *Who Speaks for the Child?* Springfield, Illinois: Charles C. Thomas, 1974.

134. SILVERMAN, CHARLES, and DAVID P. WEIKART. "Open Framework: Evolution of a Concept in Preschool Education." *High/Scope Report* 1973. Ypsilanti, Michigan: High/Scope Educational Research Foundation, 1974, pp. 14–19.

135. SKEELS, HAROLD M. *Adult Status of Children with Contrasting Early Life Experiences: A Follow-up Study*. Monograph of the Society for Research in Child Development. Chicago: University of Chicago Press, 1966.

136. SMITH, MILDRED B. "School and Home: Focus on Achievement." *Developing Programs for the Educationally Disadvantaged*. A. Harry Passow, ed. New York: Teachers College, Columbia University, 1968, pp. 89–107.

137. SMITH, NILA B. "Early Reading: Viewpoints." *Early Childhood, Crucial Years for Learning*. Edited by Margaret Rasmussen. Washington, D.C.: Association for Childhood Education International, 1966, pp. 60–64.

138. SPITZ, RENE A. *The First Year of Life: A Psychoanalytic Study of Normal and Deviant Development of Object Relations*. New York: International Universities Press, 1965.

139. ———. "The Role of Ecological Factors in Emotional Development in Infancy." *Child Development*, 1949, pp. 145–155.

140. SPOCK, BENJAMIN. *Baby and Child Care*. New York: Hawthorn Books, Inc., 1968.

141. STEVENSON, HAROLD W. In National Research Council News Release, November 4, 1971.

142. SUVIRANTA, ANNIKKI. *Home Economics Answer to the Problems Raised in Industrialized Countries*. Paper presented at the Twelfth Congress of the International Federation for Home Economics, Helsinki, Finland, July 1972.

143. TANNER, LAUREL N., and DANIEL TANNER. "News Notes." *Educational Leadership*, vol. 29 (March 1972), 6, 562.

144. THEIS, S. VAN. *How Foster Children Turn Out*. New York: State Charities Aid Association Publication No. 165, 1924.

145. TROWBRIDGE, NORMA. "Self-Concept and Socio-Economic Status in Elementary School Children." *American Educational Research Journal*, Fall 1972, pp. 525–537.

146. U. S. SENATE. *Headstart, Child Development Legislation, 1972.* S.3193 and S.3228, U. S. Senate joint hearing before the Subcommittee on Children and Youth and the Subcommittee on Employment, Manpower and Poverty of the Committee on Labor and Public Welfare. Washington, D.C., March 27, 1972.

147. VAN DEN HAAG, ERNEST. Statement in *Head Start, Child Development Legislation.* S. 3193 and S. 3228, U. S. Senate joint hearing before the Subcommittee on Children and Youth and the Subcommittee on Employment, Manpower and Poverty of the Committee on Labor and Public Welfare. Washington, D.C., March 27, 1972.

148. VANDIVIER, KERMIT. "Aircraft Brake Scandal." *Harper's Magazine*, April 1972.

149. WEAVER, GERALD N. "A Study to Determine the Approximate Age Level Most Effective for Initiating the Study of the Violin." *Lyons Music News*, November 1967.

150. WEIKART, DAVID P. In *Today's Child*, October 1971, p. 5.

151. WEPMAN, JOSEPH M. "The Modality Concept—Including a Statement of the Perceptual and Conceptual Levels of Learning." *Perception and Reading*, Proceedings of the Twelfth Annual Convention, International Reading Association, Newark, Delaware, 1968, pp. 1–6.

152. WHITE, BURTON L. "Preschool: Has It Worked?" *Compact*, July–August 1973.

153. WHITE, SHELDON H. *Report of Federal Programs for Young Children.* Cambridge, Mass: Huron Institute, 1973.

154. WIRTZ, MORVIN A. Letter to R. S. Moore, July 19, 1972.

155. YAKOVLEV, P. I. "Morphological Criteria of Growth and Maturation of the Nervous System in Man." *Mental Retardation, Proceedings of the Association for Research in Nervous and Mental Disease.* L. C. Kolb, R. L. Masland and R. E. Cooke, eds. Baltimore: Williams & Wilkins, 1962, pp. 3–46.

156. _____. Letter to R. S. Moore, July 25, 1972.

157. _____, and A. R. LECOURS. "The Myelogenetic Cycles of Regional Maturation of the Brain." *Regional Development of the Brain in Early Life.* A. Minlowski, ed. Oxford: Blackwells Scientific Publications, 1967.

158. YARROW, L. J. "Attachment and Dependency: A Developmental Perspective." *Attachment and Dependency.* J.L. Gewirtz, ed. Washington: U.H. Winston & Sons, Inc., 1972, pp.81–95.
159. YOUNG, FRANCIS. "An Evaluation of the Biological and Nearwork Concepts of Myopia Development." *American Journal of Optometry,* July 1955, pp. 354–366.
160. ZIGLER, EDWARD. "Child Care in the '70's." *Education Digest,* November 1972, pp. 17–28.
161. ———. "On Growing Up, Learning and Loving." *Human Behavior,* March 1, 1973, pp. 65–67.

Index

A Few Buttons Missing, 90
Ainsworth, Mary, 42
American Association of School Administrators, 16
American Optometric Association, 72
Ames, Dr. Louise, 27, 70, 96, 99
Andrews University, 104
anxiety, causes of, 29, 42–43, 49–50, 57, 64
arithmetic, teaching, 164, 166–167, 169, 186
Arizona, education in, 14, 22
art, teaching, 141, 158–159, 190
Ayres, A. Jean, 75

Barbrack, Christopher, 102
Bayley, Nancy, 6
Bell, Sylvia, 45
Berger, Allan S., 42–43

Birch, Dr. Harold, 74–75
Bloom, Dr. Benjamin, 5–6, 16, 77, 210
Blueprint for Survival, 205
Blumberg, Lisa, 207
Bowlby, Dr. John, 37, 41, 42, 43, 49–50, 212
brain, development of, 63–67, 80
    see also senses
breast-feeding, 117–118
Bronfenbrenner, Urie, 15
Bruner, Jerome, 77–78, 100

Cales, Queenie, 207
California, education in, 10–13
California Task Force on Early Childhood Education, 11–12, 16, 17, 18
Carpenter, Ethelouise, 209
Carter, Lowell Burney, 97

Catholic University of America, 81, 96

Chalfant, James C., 68

chores and responsibilities, teaching, 56, 57–58, 59, 92, 141–146, 162–165, 179–180, 194, 195
see also teaching

Clark, Albert, 91

Cole, Luella, 69, 72

Coleman, H. M., 70

Coleman, James, 102

Colombia University, 69

Combs, Arthur, 56

competition and group pressure, 23, 29, 176

Cornell University, 15

Czechoslovakia, preschool in, 46

Davie, Ronald, 99

Davis, H. M., 92

day-care centers
choosing, 151
costs of, 101–105
family, 14, 214
group, 46–48, 208
in Europe, 46–48, 54–55
quality of, 28, 212
see also preschool

depersonalization, 46, 104

deprived or disadvantaged children, 4, 7, 18, 23, 37–38, 40, 41–43, 48, 61, 78–79

Detroit, Michigan, 26

Dewey, John, 69

discipline, 30, 60, 115, 117, 130–131, 133–134, 148, 154–155, 175, 176, 192
see also self-discipline

Douglass, Malcolm, 86

Eagan, Walter A., 13

Ecologist, The, 205

education, see parenthood, preschool, teaching

Educational Policies Commission, 16

Elkind, David, 21, 82, 210

Emerson, Ralph Waldo, 215

Engel, Martin, 55

England, preschool in, 47–48

exercise, see physical activities

failure, coping with, 56–57

family, see home and family

feeding
during infancy, 117–120
in ages 1–3, 130, 136–138, 143
in ages 2½–5, 149–150, 155–156

Fisher, James T., 80, 90–91

Flint, Michigan, 60

Florida, education in, 14

Ford, Mrs. Helen, 104

Forester, John, 94

France, preschool in, 46

Franklin, Benjamin, 59, 183

Frostig, Marianne, 75

frustration, causes of, 29, 57, 64, 85
see also failure

Furth, Hans, 81, 84, 96

Garber, Howard, 102

gardening, 165–167, 190

Geber, Marcelle, 44

Georgia, education in, 22

Gesell, Arnold, 54, 69, 89

Gesell Institute, 27, 44, 89

Gott, Margaret, 92

Gray, Lillian, 69

Gray, Susan, 16, 17, 102

Green, Rep. Edith, 19

Grosse Pointe, Michigan, 93

Grotberg, Dr. Edith, 15

growth, *see* physical development and growth
Gumpert, David, 101

Hall, R. Vance, 98
Halliwell, Joseph, 94–95, 97
handicapped children, 3–4, 7
Harvard University, 14, 37, 39, 66, 79, 89, 101
Hawaii, education in, 14, 22
Head Start program, 41, 43–44, 45, 79
hearing, development of, 73–74, 125–126
Heber, Rick, 102
Heffernan, Helen, 95–96
Heilbroner, Robert, 205
Hendrickson, Homer, 75
Hess, Robert, 16, 99
Hilgartner, Henry, 71–72
home and family
and learning, 36–42, 55–56, 84, 87, 92
freedom from, 30
importance of, 4, 6, 15, 56, 57–58, 128, 208
obsolesence of, 5
vs. preschool, 3, 4, 9, 15, 27–30, 47, 48–51, 61, 67, 172, 208, 211
see also learning, parent-child relationship, preschool, teaching
home nursing, teaching, 199–201
Home Start program, 79, 101
Horton, Della, 102
Houston, Texas, 14
Hungary, preschool in, 46
Husén, Torsten, 97

Ilg, Dr. Frances, 69, 89, 96
imagination and fantasy, 127, 153
integrated maturity level (IML), 7, 34–35, 49, 57, 61, 80, 154, 203, 213
intersensory perception, 74–76
Israel, preschool in, 47, 54–55

Jencks, Christopher, 102
Jensen, Arthur, 6, 78–79
Johns Hopkins University, 42, 45, 102

Kagan, Jerome, 39–40, 44, 79, 83, 89
Kent State University, 209–210
King, Inez, 91–92
Krippner, Stanley, 70–71

learning
and home environment, 36–42, 55–56, 84, 87, 92
child's limitations in, 82–83
disabilities, 64, 75
during infancy, 114–116, 123–128
in ages 1–3, 130–136
in ages 2½–5, 149–170
in ages 4–7, 174–190
in ages 6–9, 193–201
in boys vs. girls, 97–99
in early vs. late starters, 88–99
natural vs. forced, 78–81
process of, 55, 63–67, 77–87, 89
see also play and playthings, senses, teaching
Lefford, Dr. Arthur, 74–75
Leonard, George B., 52
Levenstein, Phyllis, 102

Marquette, Michigan, 26
Massachusetts Institute of Technology, 205
maternal deprivation, 35, 41–42, 50

maturity levels, 7, 32–35, 49, 57, 61, 80, 89, 97, 154, 203, 213
Mawhinney, Paul, 93, 94
Meers, Dale, 8, 46–47, 48, 104
Meierhofer, Marie, 4
Metcalf, Dr. David, 65
Milkie, Dr. George, 72
Mississippi, education in, 22
Montclair, New Jersey, 94
Morency, Anne, 74
music, teaching, 56–57, 75–76
  during infancy, 125–126, 127
  in ages 1–3, 144
  in ages 2½–5, 167–168
  in ages 4–7, 184, 188–189
myelination, 65, 67

Nagera, Humberto, 38, 66
Napa County, California, 26
Nation's Schools, 22
National Academy of Science, 15
National Council of Jewish Women, 212
National Demonstration Center in Early Childhood Education, 55
National Education Association, 56
National Institute of Child Health, 42
National Institute of Mental Health, 57
National Institutes of Health, 8
New Mexico, education in, 22
New York, education in, 14
New York University, 48, 57
Newton, Frank, 71
Nimnicht, Glen, 43–44
nongraded schools, 12, 25–26, 202

Oak Ridge, Tennessee, 91
obedience, see discipline
Olson, Willard, 89

orphans, 16–17, 44
overindulgence, parental, 58–59, 60

parent-child relationship
  importance of, 3, 4, 17, 23, 28, 31, 37–45, 49–51, 56, 58–61, 116–117, 131, 133, 142, 152, 174
  rejection, 28, 39
  separation, 28, 38, 41–43, 50
    see also home and family, maternal deprivation, teaching
  parental freedom, 4–5, 6, 60
    see also working mothers
parenthood, education for, 37, 39, 61, 110, 211, 214
Paris, France, 27
Peabody University, 16, 102
pets, 167, 178
physical activities and exercise
  during infancy, 121
  in ages 1–3, 140
  in ages 4–7, 175–176
  in ages 6–9, 193, 194–195
physical development and growth
  during infancy, 112–114
  in ages 1–3, 129–130
  in ages 2½–5, 147–148
  in ages 4–7, 172–173, 175–176
  in ages 6–9, 191–192
physical punishment, 115, 130
    see also discipline
Piaget, Jean, 60, 80, 81–82, 84
play and playthings
  during infancy, 122–123
  in ages 1–3, 138–143
  in ages 2½–5, 150–151, 156–159
  in ages 4–7, 174, 178–179
  in ages 6–9, 194–195
    see also learning
Pontius, Anneliese, 57
posture, developing, 194
preschool

and politics, 6, 10–13
arguments against, 4, 7, 8–9, 13, 18–19, 22, 27–31, 37–39, 44–50, 55, 57, 61, 64, 78, 83–84, 87, 152, 171–173, 175, 203, 211, 213
arguments for, 5–6, 7, 18, 33
costs of, 101–105
in Europe, 46–48, 54–55
in various states, 10–14, 22, 71
laws regarding, 10–19, 20, 22, 26–27, 45–46, 71, 206, 211, 213–214
see also day-care centers, home and family
Prince Edward County, Virginia, 79
private property and sharing, 132, 138, 150

reading, 68–74, 85–87, 95–97, 180–181
Reichert, Dr. Conrad, 104
relocation, family, 48
responsibilities, *see* chores and responsibilities
Rich, Dorothy, 103
Riles, Dr. Wilson, 11–12, 16
Robinson, Meredith L., 80, 101
Rohwer, William, 79, 97
Rosenzweig, Mark, 67
Rosner, Dr. Jerome, 73
Rothman, Sheila, 212, 214
Ryan, Dr. Sally, 16

Sato, Dr. Tikasi, 72
Schaefer, Earl, 8, 16, 103
Scheffelin, Margaret A., 68
school, *see* formal teaching
Science Research Associates (SRA) tests, 99
self-concept and self-confidence, 38–39, 56, 57, 60, 92, 93, 142
self-discipline, 38–39, 134–135, 150, 159
senses, development of, 68–76, 115, 125–126, 172, 184, 192
see also brain
sex play, among children, 150
sharing, 132, 138, 150
Skeels, Dr. Harold, 16, 44
sleep
during infancy, 120
in ages 1–3, 130
in ages 2½–5, 148, 155
in ages 4–7, 177
Smith, Mildred, 60–61
Smith, Nila Banton, 86, 209
socialization, 23–24, 52–53, 92, 99
solitude, as childhood need, 54, 55–56
speech and language, teaching, 124, 160–162
Spitz, René, 42
Spock, Benjamin, 104
Stanford Research Institute, 80, 101
Stanford University, 16, 22
Stevenson, Harold W., 15
Sullivan, M. W., 52
Suviranta, Annikki, 62, 104

Tanner, Laurel, 53
Tavistock Clinic, 42
teaching, formal
compensatory, 79
late vs. early, 25–26, 66–67, 88–99, 202, 206–209
readiness for, 33–35, 202–203, 209–210
shortcomings of, 54, 57, 83, 88, 89
totalitarianism of, 62
see also nongraded schools, preschool
teaching, informal, 21, 53, 57, 61,

132–133, 160–170, 180–190, 195–201

arithmetic, 164, 166–167, 169, 186

art, 141, 158–159, 190

common fears regarding, 20–21, 24–27

costs of, 100–105

music, 56–57, 75–76, 125–126, 127, 144, 167–168, 184, 188–189

reading, 180–181

safety, 135, 154, 192–193, 195–196

speech and language, 124, 160–162

see also chores and responsibilities, home and family, learning

Temple University, 53

Texas, education in, 13–14, 71

Theis, S. Van, 37, 50

thumb-sucking, 120–121

U.S. Department of Health, Education and Welfare, 16, 55, 86

U.S. Division of Education of the Handicapped and Rehabilitation, 8

U.S. Interagency Council on Early Childhood Education, 15–16

U.S. Office of Child Development, 14

U.S. Senate Hearings on Head Start and Child Development, 45–46

University of California, 6, 67, 97

University of Chicago, 74

University of Colorado, 42, 65

University of Michigan, 38, 66, 89

University of North Carolina, 8, 16

University of Pittsburg, 73

University of Southern California, 75

University of Stockholm, 97

University of Wisconsin, 102

Van den Haag, Dr. Ernest, 48

vision, development of, 68–73, 125, 172, 184, 192

Wall Street Journal, 101

Washington, D.C., 8

Washington State University, 72

Wellesley College, 207

Wepman, Joseph, 74

Western Michigan University, 8

White, Burton, 37

White House Conference on Children and Youth, 58

White, Sheldon, 14, 15, 101

Whitten, Phillip, 44

Wirtz, Morvin, 8

working mothers, 4, 5, 15, 43, 45, 104, 207–208, 213–214

see also parent-child relationship

Xavier, Frances, 77

Yakovlev, Dr. Paul, 66

Yale University, 16, 84

Yarrow, L.J., 42

Young, Dr. Francis, 72–73

Zigler, Dr. Edward, 14–15, 16, 84

Zürich, Switzerland, 4